CARNIVAL, HYSTERIA,
AND WRITING

Carnival, Hysteria, and Writing

Collected Essays and Autobiography

ALLON WHITE

CLARENDON PRESS · OXFORD
1993

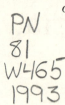

Oxford University Press, Walton Street, Oxford OX2 6DP

Oxford New York Toronto
Delhi Bombay Calcutta Madras Karachi
Kuala Lumpur Singapore Hong Kong Tokyo
Nairobi Dar es Salaam Cape Town
Melbourne Auckland Madrid

and associated companies in
Berlin Ibadan

Oxford is a trade mark of Oxford University Press

Published in the United States
by Oxford University Press Inc., New York

British Library Cataloguing in Publication Data
Data available

Library of Congress Cataloging in Publication Data
White, Allon.
Carnival, hysteria, and writing: collected essays and
autobiography / Allon White.
Includes bibliographical references and index.
1. Literature—History and criticism.   2. White, Allon.
I. Title.
PN81.W465 1993   809—dc20   92-44198
ISBN 0-19-811296-3
ISBN 0-19-812287-X (pbk)

Typeset by Hope Services (Abingdon) Ltd.
Printed in Great Britain
on acid-free paper by
Biddles Ltd.
Guildford and King's Lynn

Contents

Allon Hugh White: Chronology

1951	Born, Bedfordshire
1973	BA English, University of Birmingham
1974	MA, Centre for Cultural Studies, University of Birmingham
1974–5	Research Student, Jesus College, Cambridge
1975–6	École Pratique des Hautes Études, Paris
1976–7	Research Student, Jesus College, Cambridge
1977–8	Temporary Lecturer, School of English and American Studies, University of East Anglia
1978–80	Research Fellow, Trinity Hall, Cambridge
1979	Ph.D., University of Cambridge
1980–8	Lecturer in English, School of European Studies, University of Sussex
1981	*The Uses of Obscurity*, Routledge
1986	(with Peter Stallybrass) *The Politics and Poetics of Transgression*, Methuen
1988	Died, Brighton

For Allon White: Metaphors of Transformation

Stuart Hall

> Transgression. Perhaps one day it will seem as decisive
> for our culture, as much part of its soil, as the experi-
> ence of contradiction was at an earlier time for dialecti-
> cal thought. Transgression does not seek to oppose one
> thing to another . . . it does not transform the other
> side of the mirror . . . into a glittering expanse . . . its
> role is to measure the excessive distance that it opens at
> the heart of the limit and to trace the flashing line that
> causes the limit to arise.
>
> M. Foucault, 'Preface to Transgression', in *Language,*
> *Counter-Memory, Practice.*

There are many different kinds of metaphors in which our
thinking about cultural change takes place. These metaphors
themselves change. Those which grip our imagination, and,
for a time, govern our thinking about scenarios and possibilities of cultural transformation, give way to new metaphors,
which make us think about these difficult questions in new
terms. This essay is about one such shift which has occurred
in critical theorizing in recent years.

Metaphors of transformation must do at least two things.
They allow us to imagine what it would be like when pre-
vailing cultural values are challenged and transformed, the
old social hierarchies are overthrown, old standards and
norms disappear or are consumed in the 'festival of revolution', and new meanings and values, social and cultural con-
figurations, begin to appear. However, such metaphors must
also have analytic value. They must somehow provide ways

of thinking about the relation between the social and symbolic domains in this process of transformation. This question of how to 'think', in a non-reductionist way, the relations between 'the social' and 'the symbolic', remains the paradigm question in cultural theory—at least in all those cultural theories (and theorists) which have not settled for an elegant but empty formalism.

Classic metaphors of transformation are modelled on the 'revolutionary moment'. Terms like 'the festival of revolution' belong to that family of metaphors which has been so significant, historically, for the radical imaginary. These metaphors conceptualize the social and the symbolic or the cultural as stitched together in a relationship of rough correspondence; so that, when the social hierarchies are overthrown, a reversal of cultural values and symbols is certain sooner or later to follow. 'The ideas of the ruling class are in every epoch the ruling ideas,' Marx wrote, in a now famous (even, perhaps, infamous) passage: 'i.e. the class which is the ruling *material* force of society is at the same time its ruling *intellectual* force.' Transformation here is characteristically 'thought' in terms of reversal and substitution. When the class which 'has nothing to lose but its chains' overthrows the class 'which monopolizes the means of material and mental life', it also overthrows and substitutes alternative ideas and values in a riot of cultural transvaluation. This is the image of 'the world turned upside-down', of Trotsky's 'their morals and ours', of the mutually exclusive 'world-views' of opposing class cultures so theatrically counterposed in critics like Lukács and Goldmann, which has governed the classic metaphors of transformation. These formulations startle us now with their brutal simplicities and truncated correspondences. And yet, until recently, wherever social and symbolic or cultural transformations were thought or imagined together, it was in terms which continued to be shadowed by that metaphor.

It no longer commands assent. Cultural theory has moved decisively beyond such dramatic simplifications and binary reversals. The question is, what alternative metaphors do we have for imagining a cultural politics? Once the simplistic terms of the classic metaphors of transformation have been abandoned, do we also abandon the question of the relationship between the social and the symbolic, the 'play' between power and culture? One of the most challenging recent texts to address this question, in the wake of and fully conversant with recent critical and theoretical developments, is *The Politics and Poetics of Transgression* by Peter Stallybrass and Allon White.[1] This arresting and original book explores the persistence of the 'mapping' of cultural and social domains in Europe into the symbolic categories of 'the high' and 'the low'. The book contains a richly developed argument about how 'the carnivalesque forces, which were suppressed by bourgeois elites in their protracted withdrawal from popular culture, re-emerged in displaced and distorted form as objects of phobic disgust and repressed desire in both literature and psychopathology'; and how, 'with the emergence of a distinctively bourgeois, sanitized conception of the self in post-Renaissance European culture, various social domains were constructed as "low" and "disgusting"'.[2] I was, in fact, in the middle of rereading the volume and wondering why it had not been recognized for the 'landmark text' it is in cultural studies, when I learned of the untimely death of one of its authors, Allon White.

There are many colleagues and friends who knew Allon White more intimately or worked more closely with him than I did, and who are therefore in a much better position to speak of the quality and significance of his intellectual contribution. However, I had the pleasure and privilege to know him at an early, formative moment in his career. After his first degree in the English Department at Birmingham, he spent some time at the Centre for Cultural Studies before going on to do his Ph.D. at Cambridge, and it was during this period at the Centre that I really got to know him. He was interested in the Hegelian dialectic, especially the famous

---

[1] Peter Stallybrass and Allon White, *The Politics and Poetics of Transgression* (London, 1986).
[2] Ibid., back cover.

master–slave passages in the *Phenomenology*, and I helped to supervise his MA—that is, in so far as anyone 'supervised' him. None of us were proper Hegel scholars; he had a very clear idea of what exactly he wanted to find out and he had already developed that deceptively genial but purposeful single-mindedness which I subsequently realized characterized his work. I first learned then to admire and respect his generous, branching intelligence, his rich sense of humour, the breadth of his reading, the subtlety of his critical sensibility, and his passionate intellectual curiosity.

On the last occasion that we met, he had just recovered from another bout of illness. However, he seemed particularly well—exuberant, full of hope, brimming over with ideas. His energy dispensed a 'carnivalesque' atmosphere around the table where—in true Rabelaisian fashion—a number of his friends were having a meal together. We talked of many things, including Mikhail Bakhtin's work, which had had such a profound influence on him. When I was invited to give the first Allon White Memorial Lecture organized at Sussex University, I wanted somehow to bring together around the figure of 'carnival' these two moments in his intellectual career—his engagement with cultural studies and his rich and complex relationship to Bakhtin's work—and to reflect on some surprising and unremarked connections between them.

Bakhtin is usually assumed to have had a more profound impact on literary theory than on cultural studies and in terms of direct influence, this judgement is probably correct. However, the relationship between them with respect to Bakhtin may be closer than many people imagine. In any case, I was less concerned with tracing direct theoretical influences and more interested in 'elective affinities'—specifically, in identifying a certain theoretical shift which occurs at about the same time in a number of different but related fields of work; and where, in retrospect, the work of Bakhtin—or rather, the way Bakhtin's work was variously appropriated and reworked—proved to be of decisive value. Reading again *The Politics and Poetics of Transgression*, by

Allon White and his friend, interlocutor, and companion-at-arms, Peter Stallybrass, and thinking about the critical dialogue which the authors conduct in that book with Freud and Bakhtin about 'metaphors of transformation' and the interplay between limits and transgressions in cultural processes, a number of interesting convergences between developments in cultural theory occurring in apparently disparate domains of study at more or less the same time began to suggest themselves. The occasion of the first Allon White Memorial Lecture seemed an appropriate opportunity to reflect on them. (This text is a résumé of the talk which I gave on that occasion.)

Stallybrass and White's book takes its point of departure from Curtius's observation, in *European Literature and the Middle Ages*,[3] that the social division of citizens according to tax bands based on property calculations provided the basis for classifying the prestige and rank of literary authors and their works. 'The ranking of literary genres or authors in a hierarchy analogous to social classes is a particularly clear example of a much broader and more complex cultural process, whereby the human body, psychic forms, geographical space and the social formation all are constructed within interrelating and dependent hierarchies of high and low.'[4] This 'modelling' of the social and the cultural together according to classifications of 'high' and 'low' runs through many permutations between the moment when Curtius first observes it in late classical times and the present; but it is certainly still an active element in twentieth-century debates about the threats to civilization and 'minority culture' from the debased influences of a commercialized mass culture, which fixated the Leavises and *Scrutiny*, and in the parallel debate about 'mass culture' between the Frankfurt School and their meliorist American critics.[5] Indeed, a variant of it

[3] E. R. Curtius, *European Literature and the Middle Ages* (London, 1979).

[4] Ibid. 2.

[5] See e.g. F. R. Leavis, *Mass Civilization, Minority Culture*, repr. as app. 3 to *Education and the University* (London, 1948); Q. D. Leavis, *Fiction and the Reading Public* (London, 1932) and F. R. Leavis and Denys Thompson, *Culture and Environment* (London, 1933). For the 'mass culture' debate, see T. W. Adorno, 'Television and the Patterns of Mass Culture',

is still alive and well in the pages of the *New York Review of Books*, the *London Review of Books*, and elsewhere in the so-called debate about 'multiculturalism' and canon formation.

What Stallybrass and White register is process by which this practice of cultural classification is constantly transcoded across a variety of different domains. The nub of their argument is that

cultural categories of high and low, social and aesthetic . . . but also those of the physical body and geographical space are never entirely separable. The ranking of literary genres or authors in a hierarchy analogous to social classes is a particularly clear example of a much broader and more complex process whereby the human body, psychic forms, geographical space and the social formation are all constructed within interrelating and interdependent hierarchies of high and low. This book is an attempt to map some of these interlinked hierarchies. More particularly it attends to both the formation of those hierarchies and to the process through which the low troubles the high.[6]

Stallybrass and White's notion of 'transgression' is grounded in Bakhtin's idea of 'carnival'. 'Everywhere in literary and cultural studies today, we see "carnival" emerging as a model, as an ideal and as an analytic category.'[7] Carnival is a metaphor for the temporary licensed suspension and reversal of order, the time when the low shall be high and the high, low, the moment of upturning, of 'the world turned upside-down'. The study of Rabelais led Bakhtin to consider the existence of a whole alternative domain and aesthetic of 'the popular'. Based on studies of the importance of fairs, festivals, *mardi gras*, and other forms of popular festivity, Bakhtin uses 'carnival' to signal all those forms, tropes, and effects in which the symbolic categories of hierarchy and value are inverted. The 'carnivalesque' includes the language of the market-place—curses, profanities, oaths, colloquialisms which disrupt the privileged order of polite utterance—rituals, games, and performances, in which the genital

Dwight MacDonald, 'A Theory of Mass Culture', and Irving Howe, 'Notes on Mass Culture', all in B. Rosenberg and D. White (eds.), *Mass Culture* (Glencoe, Ill., 1956).

[6] Stallybrass and White, *The Politics and Poetics of Transgression*, 2–3.   [7] Ibid. 6.

zones, the 'material bodily lower strata', and all that belongs to them are exalted and the formal, polite forms of conduct and discourse dethroned; popular festive forms in which, for example, king or slaveholder is set aside and the fool or slave temporarily 'rules', and other occasions when the grotesque image of the body and its functions subvert the models of decorous behaviour and classical ideals.

Bakhtin's 'popular' is characterized by the practices and tropes of 'oxymoronic combination'—'doubling' in language, things wrong-side up or inside out, the bride 'weeping for laughter and laughing for tears', verbal plays and absurdities—which exploit what Bakhtin sees as the intrinsic reversibility of all symbolic order. Writing about what he calls 'unpublicized speech' and other games of conscious illogicality, Bakhtin notes that:

It is as if words had been released from the shackles of sense, to enjoy a play period of complete freedom and establish unusual relationships among themselves. True, no new consistent links are formed in most cases, but the brief coexistence of these words, expressions and objects outside the usual logical conditions discloses their inherent ambivalence. Their multiple meanings and potentialities that would not manifest themselves in normal conditions are revealed.[8]

For Bakhtin, this upturning of the symbolic order gives access to the realm of the popular—the 'below', the 'underworld', and the 'march of the uncrowned gods'. The carnivalesque also represents a connection with new sources of energy, life, and vitality—birth, copulation, abundance, fertility, excess. Indeed, it is this sense of the overflowing of libidinal energy associated with the moment of 'carnival' which makes it such a potent metaphor of social and symbolic transformation.

Frederick Jameson, in *The Political Unconscious*, notes the coexistence of two versions of the metaphors of transformation: 'the image of the triumph of the collectivity and that of the liberation of the "soul" or "spiritual body"; between a Saint-Simonian vision of social and collective engineering and

[8] Mikhail Bakhtin, *Rabelais and his World* (Bloomington, Ind., 1984), 423.

a Fourieresque Utopia of libidinal gratification; between a 1920's Leninist formulation of communism as "the Soviets plus electrification" and some more properly Marcusean 1960's celebration of an instinctual "body politic"'.[9] Bakhtin clearly belongs to the latter camp. Jameson, characteristically, establishes a priority between these two versions: 'the program of libidinal revolution is political only to the degree that it is itself a figure for social revolution'. So that, when he comes to discuss Bakhtin directly, Jameson argues that the Marxist hermeneutic—'which will . . . be defended as something like an ultimate *semantic* precondition for the intelligibility of literary and cultural texts'—takes precedence over the 'carnivalesque': the latter is made a 'local' instance of the former and Bakhtin's 'dialogic' is assimilated to and within the classic terms of the Hegelian dialectic and contradiction.[10]

In fact, what is striking and original about Bakhtin's 'carnivalesque' as a metaphor of cultural and symbolic transformation is that it is *not* simply a metaphor of inversion—setting the 'low' in the place of the 'high', while preserving the binary structure of the division between them. In Bakhtin's 'carnival', it is precisely the purity of this binary distinction which is transgressed. The low invades the high, blurring the hierarchical imposition of order; creating, not simply the triumph of one aesthetic over another, but those impure and hybrid forms of the 'grotesque'; revealing the interdependency of the low on the high and vice versa, the inextricably mixed and ambivalent nature of all cultural life, the reversibility of cultural forms, symbols, language, and meaning; and exposing the arbitrary exercise of cultural power, simplification, and exclusion which are the mechanisms upon which the construction of every limit, tradition, and canonical formation, and the operation of every hierarchical principle of cultural closure, is founded.

This seems to me to be the critical shift in the 'metaphors of transformation' which Stallybrass and White expand and

[9] Frederick Jameson, *The Political Unconscious* (London, 1981), 73.
[10] Ibid. 75.

develop in their book. As they make clear, their principal theme is 'the contradictory nature of symbolic hierarchies'. The low is thus no longer the mirror-image subject of the high, waiting in the wings to substitute it, as in the classic metaphors of revolution, but another related but different figure, which has haunted and shadowed that paradigmatic metaphor: the low as 'the site of conflicting desires and mutually incompatible representation'.

Again and again we find a striking ambivalence to the representations of the lower strata (of the body, of literature, of society, of place) in which they are both reviled and desired. Repugnance and fascination are the twin poles of the process in which a *political* imperative to reject and eliminate the debasing 'low' conflicts powerfully and unpredictably with a desire for the other.[11]

Here, far from the alternation and subordination between the two types of metaphor which Jameson sets up, we find what Jameson calls the 'metaphysic of desire' and transgression invading, subverting, and complexifying irretrievably the binary terms of the more classic forms of the metaphor.

What struck me forcibly in rereading *The Politics and Poetics of Transgression* is that this process of shifting between two related but increasingly different metaphors of transformation is no merely 'local' interpretive insight by the two authors, but symptomatic of a major transition in our cultural and political life, as well as in critical theoretical work in recent decades. It is here that certain 'elective affinities' with work in cultural theory at the Centre for Cultural Studies in the 1970s began to suggest themselves.

By way of illustration, we can take three examples: the first from the cultural debates which belong to the 'founding moment' (*sic*) of cultural studies; the second from work on youth subcultures and the popular; the third from the analysis of ideological discourse.

It is not often recalled that cultural studies 'began' at Birmingham with an interrogation of the high/low categories of the cultural debate. It inherited these terms in part from

[11] Stallybrass and White, *The Politics and Poetics of Transgression*, 5.

the Leavisite preoccupation with the disappearance of a 'living' organic popular culture in the eighteenth century and its replacement by a debased 'mass civilization' offering a serious threat to 'minority culture'; in part from the debate about 'mass culture' between conservative and demotic cultural critics, which is where so-called 'media studies' began.[12] In fact, cultural studies defined itself critically in relation to the terms of both these debates. It rejected the essentially élitist cultural programme in which the *Scrutiny* critique was grounded; and it rejected the either/ors of the 'mass culture' debate.[13] It sought to disentangle the question of the intrinsic literary and cultural value of particular texts from the practice of cultural classification—an elementary distinction which, regrettably, highly sophisticated contributors to the current 'canon' debate seem incapable of making. (Sociology often deserves its bad name; but a little sociological sophistication would not go amiss here and there.)

Raymond Williams's analysis of the operation of the 'selective tradition' and his later deconstruction of 'literature' into modes of writing took on a subversive charge in the context of the same debate.[14] For others of us, it was the category of 'the popular' which effectively cut the Gordian knot—not through an uncritically populist celebration, which has been common in some circles, but because of the way it disturbed the settled contours and—precisely—transgressed the boundaries of cultural classification. Since the rise of modernism, and even more in the era of 'post-modernism', it is impossible to keep the high and the low carefully segregated into their proper places in the classifying scheme. We tried to find a way out of the binary fix by rethinking 'the popular', not in terms of fixed qualities or a given content, but *relationally*—as those forms and practices which are excluded from, and opposed to, the 'valued', the canon,

---

[12] For a summary which locates the origins of media studies in the 'mass culture' debate, see Leon Bramson, *The Political Context of Sociology* (Princeton, NJ, 1961), ch. 6.

[13] For an early attempt to break out of this binary fix, see S. Hall and P. Whannel, *The Popular Arts* (London, 1964).

[14] See, *inter alia*, Raymond Williams, 'The Analysis of Culture', in *The Long Revolution* (Harmondsworth, 1965); and *Marxism and Literature* (Oxford, 1977).

through the operation of symbolic practices of exclusion and closure.[15]

In 1975, the Centre published a volume of essays on *Youth Sub-cultures in Post-war Britain*. Though this volume became quite influential in the field, setting in motion a number of further studies, it represented a very crude beginning and it is cited here not to rescue it from comparative obscurity but because of what it tells us about how ideas of transgression, symbolic reversal, and cultural contestation were being reconceptualized.

The book was entitled *Resistance through Rituals*: the use of the two terms in its title was deliberate.[16] 'Resistance' signalled those forms of disaffiliation (like the new social movements associated with youth) which were in some sense challenges to and negotiations of the dominant order but which could not be assimilated to the traditional categories of revolutionary class struggle. 'Rituals' pointed to the symbolic dimension of these movements—the stylization of social actions, the 'play' of signs and symbols, the 'playing out' of resistance and repetition in the theatres of everyday life, the 'bricoleur effect', as fragments and emblems were dissociated from one cultural discourse and reassembled in another. It also hinted at an answer to the question, posed by many conventional social critics, whether there were built-in limits to all such forms of resistance—because of their gestural quality, their dissociation from the classic agencies of social transformation, their status—as it was put in the language of

---

[15] This is the position I advanced in 'Notes towards Deconstructing "The Popular"', in Raphael Samuel (ed.), *People's History and Socialist Theory* (London, 1981). What is meant by a 'relational' approach to this process of cultural classification is best suggested by an example. In the 18th century, the novel was regarded as a 'low' and vulgar form. In the 20th century, the 18th-century novel has become a touchstone of 'serious' literature. Nevertheless, new novels continue to be ranked according to some implicit high/low, serious/popular generic distinction. The contents of the categories have changed, but the practice of mapping literature within a 'system of differences' remains. What matters is how 'high' is defined, at any historical moment, in relation to 'low', not these categories as fixed, with respect to either their contents or their transcendental cultural value. The point is rudimentary with respect to such studies of 'symbolic classification' as Levi-Strauss's *Mythologies: The Origin of Table Manners* (New York, 1978), Mary Douglas's *Purity and Danger* (London, 1966), and V. W. Turner's *The Ritual Process* (Ithaca, NY, 1977), all referred to in Stallybrass and White, *The Politics and Poetics of Transgression*.

[16] S. Hall and T. Jefferson (eds.), *Resistance through Rituals* (London, 1976).

the time—as 'magical solutions'. This is a serious question—
Bakhtin himself acknowledged that 'no consistent links are
formed in most cases'—but this way of putting it also
reflected the lingering presence of the belief that the symbolic
could not be anything but a second-order, dependent category.

In the context of this discussion, what seems most significant now is the way *Resistance through Rituals* actively dis-
tanced itself from the classical metaphors of 'revolutionary
struggle' and the reform/revolution antinomies by offering in
their place an *expanded* definition of social rupture. In place
of the simple binaries of 'the class struggle', it substituted the
Gramscian notion of 'repertoires of resistance' which, it
insisted, were always conjuncturally defined and historically
specific. It attempted to ground these repertoires, not directly
in the either/ors of classical class conflict but in an analysis
of the 'balance in the relations of forces' developed by
Gramsci in his analysis of hegemonic struggle.

Negotiation, resistance, struggle: the relations between a subordinate and a dominant cultural formation, wherever they fall in this
spectrum, are always intensely active, always oppositional in a
structural sense (even when this 'opposition' is latent, or experienced simply as the normal state of affairs . . .). Their outcome is
not given but made. The subordinate class brings to this 'theatre of
struggle' a repertoire of strategies and responses—ways of coping as
well as ways of resisting. Each 'strategy' in the repertoire mobilizes
certain material, social [and symbolic] elements: it constructs these
into the supports for the different ways the class lives, [negotiates,]
and resists its continuing subordination. Not all the strategies are of
equal weight; not all are potentially counter-hegemonic.[17]

This is a very early stage in the formulation of this problem, and the traces of a kind of 'class reductionism' are still
to be found in it.[18] But its interest lies in the way notions of a
variety of forms of resistance replace the primacy of 'the class

---

[17] *Resistance through Rituals*, 44.
[18] Rosalind Coward elaborated this charge of 'class reductionism' in 'Class, "Culture"
and the Social Formation', in *Screen*, 18/1 (Spring 1977); see also, the reply by I. Chambers,
J. Clarke, Iain Chambers, John Clarke, Ian Connell, Lidia Curti, Stuart Hall, and Tony
Jefferson, 'Marxism and Culture', *Screen*, 18/4 (Winter 1977–8).

struggle'; in the movement towards a less determinist, more conjunctural way of understanding the 'repertoires of resistance' and the centrality it gave to the symbolic dimension. Gramsci is the most significant theoretical influence on these formulations. It was his concept of the 'national-popular' as a terrain of cultural and hegemonic struggle 'relatively autonomous' at least of other types of social struggle which helped us to displace the traces of reductionism in the argument.

The third example is from the analysis of ideological discourse. A great deal of attention was given in the 1970s at the Centre for Cultural Studies to trying to rethink and rework the conceptual categories of ideology, its mechanisms, and mappings in a number of different areas. This work was conducted within a specific conceptual space, defined by a number of theoretical axes: first, by the radical absence of an adequate theory or conceptualization of language and the ideological in Marx's writing and, particularly, the need to transcend the 'base–superstructure' metaphor; secondly, in relation to the attempts in what we can broadly define as the 'Althusserian School', to supply the absent theoretical framework; thirdly, face to face with the new theories of language and the semiotic which had begun to transform the ground of cultural theory; fourthly, the inadequacies of available theorizations for thinking together, in any convincing or concrete way, the relations between the 'social' and the 'symbolic'.[19]

Gramsci was important here too. But the key text undoubtedly was *Marxism and the Philosophy of Language*, by V. N. Volosinov, which the Seminar Press published in English in 1973 and which had a decisive and far-reaching impact on our work.[20] First, it established the definitively discursive character of ideology. 'The domain of ideology coincides with the domain of signs,' Volosinov wrote. 'They equate with one another. Whenever a sign is present,

---

[19] For an account of the work on this area during this period, see S. Hall, D. Hobson, A. Lowe, and P. Willis (eds.), *Culture, Media, Language* (London, 1980).

[20] V. N. Volosinov, *Marxism and the Philosophy of Language* (New York, 1973).

ideology is present too. Every ideological process possesses semiotic value.'

Secondly, it marked the decisive breaking of the correspondence between classes and the idea of separate, autonomous, and self-sufficient 'class languages', ideological universes, or, to use Lukácsian language, 'world-views'. 'Class does not coincide with the sign-community, i.e. with the community which is the totality of users of the same sets of signs for ideological communication. Thus various classes will use the same language. As a result, differently oriented accents intersect in every ideological sign. Sign becomes the arena of class struggle.'[21]

Thirdly, it advanced the key argument that, since different accents coincide within the same sign, the struggle over meaning did not take the form of substituting one, self-sufficient class language for another, but of the disarticulation and rearticulation of different ideological accentings within the same sign. It followed that meaning cannot be finally fixed, that every ideological sign, as Volosinov put it, is 'multi-accentual'; and consequently that this continuous discursive 'play' or shifting of meaning within language was the condition of possibility of ideological contestation. 'A sign that has been withdrawn from the pressure of the social struggle inevitably loses force, degenerating into allegory and becoming the object, not of a live social intelligibility, but of a mere philological comprehension.'[22] Another way of putting it would be to acknowledge the infinite reversibility of the 'logics' of ideological discourse, which are so much more governed by the 'laws' of displacement and condensation of Freud's dream-work than of Enlightenment reason. 'The living ideological sign is Janus-faced'; and this 'inner dialectic quality of the sign' is present in the 'ordinary conditions of life' but particularly relevant 'in times of social crisis and revolutionary change'.[23]

Fourthly, *Marxism and the Philosophy of Language* made us see with clarity that what an ideology 'does', so to speak,

---

[21] *Marxism and the Philosophy of Language*, 10, 23.   [22] Ibid. 23.   [23] Ibid.

is not to impose an already formed class perspective on another, less powerful one, but rather to intervene in the dialogic fluidity of language, to effect the 'cut' of ideology across language's infinite semiotic 'play', to define the limits and regulative order of a 'discursive formation' in order to attempt, arbitrarily, to fix the flow of language, to stabilize, freeze, suture language to a univocal meaning. 'The very same thing that makes the ideological sign vital and mutable is also however that which makes it a refracting and distorting medium. The ruling class strives to impart a superclass, eternal character to the ideological sign, to extinguish or drive inward the struggle between social value judgements which occurs in it, to make the sign uniaccentual.'[24] In Volosinov's view, every linguistic formation consists, in fact, of 'genre, register, sociolect, dialect, and the mutual interanimation of these forms', to use Allon White's phrase.[25]

Marxism and the Philosophy of Language therefore played a critical role in the general theoretical shift from any lingering flirtation with even a modified version of the 'base–superstructure' metaphor to a fully discourse-and-power conception of the ideological.[26] And yet, there was something of great significance about that text which we did *not* understand at the time. In fact, these important formulations about the multi-accentuality of the ideological sign and the struggle to contest and shift meanings—of meaning as the symbolic stake in all social antagonism—belonged to and derived their theoretical and metaphorical power from a wider philosophical context. Volosinov's prescriptions, which we tended to read rather 'technically', required to be 'read' intertextually—in the context of a broader model or set of metaphors about social change: specifically in relation to Bakhtin's *dialogic principle* and the great themes of 'the carnival'. Volosinov's account counterposed the exercise of cultural power through the imposition of the norm in an attempt to freeze and fix meaning in language to the constant eruption of new

---

[24] Ibid. [25] See Ch. 7.
[26] This is acknowledged in, for example, S. Hall, 'The Problem of Ideology: Marxism without Guarantees', in Betty Matthews (ed.), *Marx: A Hundred Years On* (London, 1983).

meanings, the fluidity of heteroglossia, and the way meaning's inherent instability and heterogeneity dislocated and displaced language's apparently 'finished' character. But this
account mirrored, in miniature, Bakhtin's 'carnival', with its
image of the medieval cosmology of the world, ordered into
top and bottom, higher and lower, along the vertical line—
'the surprisingly consistent vertical character which projects
everything upwards and out of time's movement'—and of the
way this comes to be countered by the 'downward' thrust of
the popular, the encroachment of the 'world's horizontal',
which not only puts another time and space in play, but relativizes that which represented itself as absolute and complete.

The reason we missed these deeper metaphoric reverbera-
tions of Volosinov's textual argument is that, though we
knew that Volosinov had been a member of the Bakhtin circle, we did not at that time fully appreciate the complexity
of the problem, as yet not satisfactorily resolved, of who the
'real' author of *Marxism and the Philosophy of Language*
actually was. Was the text written by Volosinov, who was a
gifted linguist, fully capable of writing such a work? Or was
it jointly authored by Bakhtin and Volosinov? Or—as many
now   believe—was   it   Bakhtin's   text   published   under
Volosinov's name or Bakhtin's text added to and emended by
Volosinov? Critics are now familiar with this complex story
of the disputed texts of Bakhtin's; of the circle of brilliant
intellectuals in Russia in the 1920s who closely collaborated,
argued, and debated these literary, linguistic, and philosophical questions in an intense period of dialogic discussion over
many years.[27]

Indeed the irony did not end there. For Bakhtin had a
brother, Nikolai, who had been Mikhail's *alter ego* in their
early lives, with whom he shared not only many common
ideas but an intense personal relationship—'the same enmity
will touch two different souls, my enemy and brother'—and
who was separated from him during the Revolution. Nikolai
had not only become a member of the Wittgenstein circle in

---

[27] See the account of the Bakhtin circle in K. Clark and M. Holquist, *Mikhail Bakhtin*
(Cambridge, Mass., 1984).

Cambridge but taught for many years at Birmingham University (1939–50). He had been attracted to the university by his friendship with two former Cambridge associates now teaching there—George Thompson, the Professor of Classics, and the Professor of German, Roy Pascal, who was *inter alia* a firm friend, ally, and supporter of the Centre for Cultural Studies—and was later to found the university's Linguistics Department.[28]

In their book *Mikhail Bakhtin*, Clark and Holquist are firmly of the view that Bakhtin was the author of both *Marxism and the Philosophy of Language* and *Freudianism: A Critical Sketch*, hitherto also attributed to Volosinov; and this was confirmed by many members of the circle, including Bakhtin's widow. However, as is now well known, Bakhtin refused to sign the document which was prepared, at his request, in 1975, to clarify the question of authorship, and as his manuscripts and papers have all been destroyed, the issue is unlikely ever to be finally resolved.[29]

This 'mystery' about authorship has its deeply serious side, for it has to be placed in the context of the threat to unorthodox intellectual work, as the Stalinist gloom gathered, and Bakhtin's retreat into anonymity, culminating in his arrest and exile for religious activities. But, as is always the case with Bakhtin, this tragic aspect is 'doubled' by its parodic, carnivalesque aspect; for it has also to be understood in the context of the love of pranks, games, verbal wit, ingenuity, and play amongst the Bakhtin circle and of the principles and theories of 'the dialogic' and heteroglossia which governed both the philosophical speculations and the intellectual exchanges of its members. According to the dialogic principle, the self is constituted only through its relationship to the other, all understanding is dialogic in nature, 'meaning belongs to a word in its position between speakers',

[28] See the introduction by A. Duncan Jones to N. Bakhtin's *Lectures and Essays* (Birmingham, 1963). The Birmingham connection is fully described in Clark and Holquist, *Mikhail Bakhtin*. It, and the existence of a Bakhtin archive in the university library, were first brought to my notice by Professor Peter Davidson. For the relationship between these different figures in the Wittgenstein circle, see T. Eagleton, 'Wittgenstein's Friends', in *Against the Grain* (London, 1986).

[29] See Clark and Holquist, *Mikhail Bakhtin*, ch. 10.

and agreement between collaborators in the dialogic relationship is defined as 'co-voicing'. Bakhtin had meditated on the
'question of authorship', the shifting relations between I and
other, reported speech, and the politics of quotation in as
early a text as the unfinished *Architectonics of Answerability*,
and they continued to be themes of his later work.
Dialogism, as Clark and Holquist observe, 'celebrates altereity . . . As the world needs my altereity to give it meaning, I
need the authority of others to define, or author, my self'.[30]
In retrospect, it would have been very surprising if questions
of who 'owned' which ideas in *Marxism and the Philosophy
of Language* turned out to be a simple matter amongst
Bakhtin and his co-voicers.

Lacking the principle of the dialogic in its fullness, we
tended to appropriate 'Volosinov' more narrowly—to supply
the basis for rethinking the relations between language and
social transformation in a non-reductionist way. We thought
of this exercise as, in some way, a recovery of a 'dialectical'
perspective. As we have noted, this is also the context in
which Frederick Jameson appropriates and inflects Bakhtin in
his development of a Marxist hermeneutics in *The Political
Unconscious*. In retrospect, this significantly underplays what
is happening in the shift of metaphors from 'the dialectic of
class antagonism' to the 'dialogic of multi-accentuality'.
These two logics are not mutually exclusive. But nor are they
subsumable into or substitutable for one another in this way.
Where, classically, the terms of the dialectic grounds the
complex supersession of different social forces, providing it
with its governing logic, its meta-narrative, the dialogic
emphasizes the shifting terms of antagonism, the intersection
of different 'accentings' in the same discursive terrain, rather
than the dialectical 'parting of the ways'. It rigorously
exposes the absence of a guaranteed logic or 'law' to the play
of meaning, the endlessly shifting positionalities of the
places of enunciation, as contrasted with the 'given' positions
of class antagonism, classically conceived. The notion of

articulation/disarticulation interrupts the Manichaeism or the binary fixity of the logic of class struggle, in its classic conception, as the archetypal figure of transformation. The dialogic intrudes the idea of reversibility, of historic shifts which bear the traces of the past indelibly inscribed into the future, of the rupture of novelty which is also and always caught up in the return of the archaic . . .

One is reminded here of Gramsci's rethinking of the nature of the revolutionary moment in its generic form in the light of the experience of Caesarism. *A* does not defeat *B* or *B* defeat *A*, with each having the self-sufficient character of 'a generically progressive and generically reactionary force'. Instead, both are caught up, in modern times, in the what Gramsci calls the 'dialectic [of] revolution/restoration'.[31] Here destruction has to be conceived, not mechanically but as an active process: 'destruction/reconstruction'. These oxymoronic formulations, which capture the dialogic relationship between antagonistic forces, prefigure Gramsci's historic transition from a 'war of manœuvre' to a 'war of position'—another important shift of the metaphors of transformation which had its impact on critical theorizing at the same moment and which was pointing in the same direction.

It is difficult to capture—except 'metaphorically'—what this shift of the metaphors of transformation consists of. It is certainly not the simple rejection of one type of metaphor and the substitution of another, 'better' (i.e. more theoretically correct) one. It is more a question of being caught on the meridian between two variants of the same idea; of being suspended between the metaphors—of leaving the one without being able to transcend it, and of moving towards the other without being fully able to encompass it. What the so-called shift to the 'dialogic' seems to involve is the 'spatialization' of moments of conflict and antagonism which have hitherto been captured by metaphors of condensation. The dialogic has given up on any pure idea of transcendence. Rather, it suggests that, within every moment of reversal,

---

[31] A. Gramsci, 'State and Civil Society', in *The Prison Notebooks* (London, 1971), 219 ff.

there is always the surreptitious return of the trace of the past; within any rupture are the surprising effects of reduplication, repetition, and ambivalence. The insertion of ambivalence and ambiguity into the 'space' of the condensed metaphors of reversal and transcendence is, I believe, the guiding thread to the incomplete displacements which seem to be in progress in this movement within the metaphorical discourse. Certainly, the 'dialogic' does not refuse the idea of antagonism. But it obliges us always to think of antagonism as more or less than a 'pure' moment; to redefine the 'carnivalesque' in terms of an economy of excess, surplus, and supplementarity, on the one hand, or of underdetermination, absence, and lack, on the other. None of the metaphors of transformation, which contain elements of 'the festival of the oppressed', of 'the world turned upside-down' within them, when rephrased within the perspective of the 'dialogic', can produce a fully adequate representation of the poles of the antagonism they are attempting to encompass or represent. There is always something not accounted for, or left over. Like the symptoms and representations of psychic life, they are destined to be either over- or underdetermined. The reference to the model of 'the symptom' is not casual. The argument here has been advanced mainly in relation to Bakhtin. But in Stallybrass and White's book, as so often elsewhere, the figure of Freud and the discourse of psychoanalysis have proved to be equally decisive elements in bringing about the shift.

These were some of the inchoately expressed and formulated ideas which began, slowly and unevenly, to transform the theoretical terms and the shaping metaphors of work in cultural studies during the 1970s. *The Politics and Poetics of Transgression*, definitively a book of the 1980s, is several theoretical turns beyond these halting movements. But it seems to me a turn of the same screw. The parallels and 'elective affinities' come through strongly as soon as one examines how Stallybrass and White set out to rework and expand Bakhtin. What is particularly striking is their capacity to work *with* and at the same time to work *on* Bakhtin's

'carnival' metaphor, genuinely inhabiting its richly connota-
tive possibilities, taking seriously the critiques advanced
against it (its binaryism, its 'utopian populism') while at the
same time transforming it. This is exemplary theoretical
work, which needs to be sharply contrasted with the many
examples we have of current theoretical work, which mainly
consists of ventriloquizing 'their masters' voices'. As a result,
the authors seem to be justified in arguing that 'It is only by
completely shifting the grounds of the debate, by transforming the "problematic" of carnival' that 'carnival' can be
shown to be simply 'one instance of a generalized economy
of transgression and of the recoding of high/low relations
across the whole social structure'.[32] It is precisely their success in 'building upon the work of Bakhtin but attempting to
avoid the limitations identified in his work' which provides
us with the measure of the significance of the 'intervention in
the current surge of Bakhtin inspired studies' which *The
Politics and Poetics of Transgression* represents.

Typically, the critiques of the binary-and-inversion structure of the classic metaphors of transformation have been
followed by ditching them in favour of more lateral or horizontal metaphors—a movement now so fashionable in critical theory as almost to have acquired the status of the banal.
This is certainly the fate which has befallen the so-called
high/low distinction in the debate about popular culture.
Colin McCabe, for example, is certainly correct in his polem-
ical essay 'Defining Popular Culture' to draw attention to the
importance of 'the complex ways in which traditions and
technologies combine to produce audiences' and to argue
that 'this figuring of different audiences' radically cuts across
and disrupts the positions of the champions of high art and
popular culture alike.[33] He is certainly right to note the way
Gramsci's idea of 'the national popular', which did so much
to transform the debate about 'the popular' in the 1970s,
transcends the class-against-class ways of reading culture

[32] Stallybrass and White, *The Politics and Poetics of Transgression*, 19.
[33] Colin McCabe, 'Defining Popular Culture', in McCabe (ed.), *High Theory/Low Culture* (Manchester, 1986), 8.

which, as he says, debilitated the European left. He may indeed have a point in saying that nevertheless Gramsci remains in some way imprisoned by the Hegelian–Marxist theory of culture from which he is trying to escape. McCabe may also be right in dismissing the alternative (which I advanced in 'Deconstructing "The Popular"'), where, according to McCabe, 'the social is theorized as overlapping terrains of struggle and popular culture is simply a way of specifying areas of resistance to dominant ideological forms'.[34] This, he says, 'through however many million mediations' reproduces the very weakness of the position whose problems it is striving to repair.[35]

The only alternative, it seems, is simply to abandon it. 'What seems positive to me in the commitment to popular culture', he argues, 'is that element which is determined to break with any and all of the formulations which depend on a high/low, elite/mass distinction.'[36] John Caughie, who adds to McCabe's argument such important considerations as 'the discrimination of pleasure and an understanding of the enormous machineries of desire which are caught up in the circulation of the popular', comes to the same conclusion in a later essay in the same volume.[37]

One can only respond that it depends on what you mean by abandoning it. Putting it 'under erasure', as Derrida would say, yes. Abandoning it altogether, no. Certainly the high/low distinction is not—has never been—tenable in the naturalistic, transhistorical terms in which it has been advanced. But if the proposition is that by 'abandoning it' one will have transcended the problem to which it referred—Stallybrass and White's persistent tendency for European culture to map 'the human body, psychic forms, geographical space and the social formation . . . within interrelating and interdependent hierarchies of high and low'—then one must doubt the strategy.

[34] *High Theory/Low Culture*, 4.
[35] Ibid. However, 'Deconstructing "The Popular"' is not an essay about and does not use the concept of 'mediations'.
[36] 'Deconstructing "The Popular"', 8.
[37] John Caughie, 'Popular Culture: Notes and Revisions', in McCabe (ed.), *High Theory/Low Culture*.

Stallybrass and White, at any rate, do *not* move in that way. Rather, they take the processes of ranking and classification which these axes of high and low represent as fundamental cultural processes, critical within European culture for the constitution of the identity of any cultural domain. The concepts of ambivalence, hybridity, interdependence, which, we have argued, began to disrupt and transgress the stability of the hierarchical binary ordering of the cultural field into high and low, *do not destroy the force of the operation of the hierarchical principle in culture*, any more, it may be said, than the fact that 'race' is not a valid scientific category 'in any way undermines its symbolic and social effectuality'.[38] High and low may not have the canonical status claimed for them; but they remain fundamental to the way cultural practices are organized and regulated. What 'displacing them' means is not abandoning them but shifting the focus of theoretical attention from the categories 'in themselves' as repositories of cultural value to the process of cultural classification itself. It reveals these cultural hierarchies as *necessarily arbitrary*—as an attempt, transcoded from one domain to another, to fix, stabilize, and regulate a 'culture' in hierarchical ascending order, using all the metaphorical force of the 'above' and the 'below'.

The classification of cultural domains into the self-sufficient and apparently transcendental distinctions of high and low is revealed, by the operation of the carnivalesque, and by the transgressions of pleasure, play, and desire, as an exercise in cultural regulation, designed to make cultural practices into a *formation* which can then be sustained in a binary form by strategies of cultural power. The fact that the cultural field cannot be stabilized in this way does not prevent the exercise in boundary construction being attempted again, in another place, for another time. Cultural practices are never outside the play of power. And one way in which power operates in the apparently decentred sphere of culture is through the struggle to harness it, to superimpose on it, to

---

[38] Introduction to J. Donald and A. Rattansi (eds.), 'Race', in *Culture and Difference* (London, 1992), 3.

regulate and enclose its diverse and transgressive forms and energies, within the structure and logic of a normative or canonical binary. This cultural operation, as I tried to argue elsewhere,[39] is always in some way linked—and continues, even in our more diversified post-modern culture, to be linked—with the mechanisms of cultural hegemony.[40] One would have to be extremely naïve to believe that the current controversies around 'multiculturalism' and the canon—contemporary form of the high/low cultural debate—is a disinterested conversation between scholars, unrelated to questions of cultural authority or to containing the transgressive danger of social, ethnic, gendered, and sexual hybridity.

This argument is advanced with great clarity in Stallybrass and White's conclusion:

We have had cause throughout this book to reflect on an unnoticed slide between two quite distinct kinds of 'grotesque', the grotesque of the 'Other' of the defining group or self, and the grotesque as a boundary phenomenon of hybridization or inmixing, in which self and other become enmeshed in an inclusive, heterogeneous, dangerously unstable zone. What starts as a *simple* repulsion or rejection of symbolic matter foreign to the self inaugurates a process of introjection and negation which is always *complex* in its effects. In order to fathom this complexity, this inner dynamic of the boundary constructions necessary to collective identity, we have to avoid conflating the two different forms of the grotesque. If the two are confused, it becomes impossible to see that a fundamental mechanism of identity formation *produces* the second, hybrid grotesque at the level of the political unconscious by the very struggle to exclude the first . . . The point is that the *exclusion* necessary to the formation of social identity at level one is simultaneously a *production* at the level of the Imaginary, and a production, what is more, of a complex hybrid fantasy emerging out of the very attempt to demarcate boundaries, to unite and purify the social collectivity . . . The general processes of classification which bear most closely upon the identity of the collectivity are indissociable from the heterodox

---

[39] 'Deconstructing "The Popular"'.

[40] The argument in S. Hall, 'Deconstructing "The Popular"', is that to see the classification of culture into 'high/low' as related to the struggle over hegemony does not require either fetishizing the content of each category or a class correspondence way of reading the relationship between the social and the symbolic.

symbolic material of the Imaginary. The unconscious is to this extent *necessarily* a political unconscious as Jameson avers, for the exclusion of other social groups and classes in the struggle to achieve categorical self-identity appears as a special dialogism, an agon of voices—sometimes even an *argument*—within the shared Imaginary of the class in question. The very drive to achieve a singularity of collective identity is simultaneously productive of unconscious heterogeneity, with its variety of hybrid figures, competing sovereignties and exorbitant demands.[41]

'What is socially peripheral may be symbolically central.'[42] The movement from simple binary metaphors of cultural and symbolic transformation to the more complex figures described above represents an absolutely fundamental 'turn' in cultural theory, mappable in a number of different fields. *The Politics and Poetics of Transgression* represents an exemplary instance of this general movement; and the contribution which Allon White was able to make to it, in the tragically brief period of his working and writing life, is only just beginning, retrospectively, to be properly understood.

[41] Stallybrass and White, *The Politics and Poetics of Transgression*, 193–4.
[42] Ibid. 23; quoted from B. Babcock, *The Reversible World* (Ithaca, NY, 1978), 32.

1 *Too Close to the Bone:*
Fragments of an Autobiography

Faust, despairing of all philosophies, may yet drain a
marsh or rescue some acres from the sea.

> (Edward Dowden)
> Passionate art, the drowner of dykes . . .
> (W. B. Yeats)

I suppose this is my biography, my life. Fragments of memory. Perhaps even a memorial. Except that I don't believe in
biographies and advise you to be especially sceptical about
this one, written, one has to say, under the stress of illness
and in extreme haste. Self-perception is distorted enough in
the healthy, God knows what it is like in those gripped by
terminal illness. Don't ask me: I'm terminally ill.

I am 36 years old, a teacher of literature, and I am dying
of leukaemia. I have fought the thing for two years, I have
had two bone-marrow transplants from my sister and more
chemotherapy than anyone should ever have to endure. But it
seems I am losing the battle now. Flaccid, diseased cells are
swarming and swelling inside my bones and I have little time
left. Of course I've waited too long before writing this and
now it is late, probably too late. Like beginning to write at
twilight with no lamp as the darkness falls. And there is no
light now. There was some a little while ago and I should
have written then. I also had some within me, a deep blue
light the colour of Iris which now and then I could see far
inside my body and which glowed and gave me great com-
fort. But it is really dark now, my blue light has deserted me
and it is getting very late.

First published simultaneously in Britain and the USA in the *London Review of Books*, 4
May 1989, and *Raritan Review*, 8 (Spring 1989); repr. in book form by the *London Review of
Books* (1991).

An Old Novel

Several things still puzzle me. I will tell you about the novel and you will have to see what you think—I know that a central knot of my life and unconscious world is tied up in that abortive fiction, but I cannot quite touch it myself. Perhaps the roots of my illness are there in that early attempt to write a novel. Certainly it now seems like it, years later.

It was when I was breaking up with my first wife. One night I was in my room in Norwich (I had been teaching away from home at the University there) and, pained beyond endurance by the break-up, I suddenly began to write—*in extremis*, you might say (it seems it takes cataclysm to get me to write anything other than scholarly articles). I began to write fast and fluently, pages of the stuff, and though my eyes were full of tears and I normally write with pedantic care and exquisite self-consciousness, this time a coherent story sprang from the end of my pen already formed, the fictional names and the narrative all in place without my conscious mind having any idea that all this had been waiting inside me. In fact, this story, or another story of which this was a strange and displaced version, had been waiting thirty years for its expression, but I was not to discover that until much later. At the time, all I knew was this plangent ecstasy of automatic writing in which a clear, sad story poured out of me, one which I had never known was there.

Even now, as I resume the story for you, new connections come to mind, but they will have to wait a while. The plot was a double-braid: one strand was set in the 17th century during the Civil War and concerned an obsessive, self-absorbed mystic called Nicodemus; the other strand was set in the late 1950s in Sardinia and concerned a hydraulics engineer called Lucas Arnow employed by the Ford Foundation to drain the malarial swamps of the Sardinian coast as part of the world-wide effort after the last war to eradicate malaria. God knows where these names and characters came from, but they wrote themselves immediately onto the pages in front of me and I was surprised to meet them. I knew immediately that they were dissociated and egoistic bits of myself split by time and place, but they were also bizarre and unexpected, complete strangers to me. I didn't even know I knew about the Ford Foundation project, but evidently I did because it is perfectly accurate—I must have read it some-where and 'forgotten'. I think this kind of forgetfulness, this false forgetfulness where things are lost but not destroyed, hidden but perhaps not for ever, is what this unconventional biography means by 'memory'. Not so much memories as things forgotten and found again. Remembrance.

Anyway, Nicodemus, my 17th-century religious fanatic, was making his way from the Midlands to the Fens—to Ely, in fact, because he had a vision that the fenland marshes were the place of salvation. He had concocted a bizarre and idiosyncratic theology, rather like the wonderful Miller in *The Cheese and the Worms*, but in his case it was marshland, and particularly the reeds, which played the central part. The reed is one of the symbols of the Passion, for, on the Cross, Christ had been tendered a vinegar-soaked sponge on the end of a reed. The reed also represents the Just, who dwell on the banks of the waters of Grace. And it represents the mul-titude of the lowly faithful ('Can the rush grow up without mire? Can the flag grow without water?'). The Evangelists wrote with reeds upon papyrus, another kind of reed bearing the words of God. And the Red Sea (actually Yam Suph, the Reed Sea) had parted to lead the way to the Promised Land. From these and other scraps of insignificant material Nicode-mus had stitched together his passionate, crazy faith, and it was now leading him on a pilgrimage, amidst the carnage of the Civil War, to Ely and the Great Fens.

His half of the story was thoroughly picaresque. It was farcical—a bit of a carnival I would say now, but I hadn't read about Bakhtin and the carnivalesque in those days (it was 1977). Nicodemus gradually accumulated a motley gang of misfits and outcasts on his slow pilgrimage, including Widow Joan, a vast and wonderful creation, who, in one episode, shows her contempt for a local vicar (who has objected to their overnight stay in his parish) by baptizing a huge, squealing pig in the village pond. I forget the other details of this 17th-century part of the plot, which essentially creaked and reeled from one improbable village adventure to another until Nicodemus, having lost all his friends and hangers-on, arrives alone at the Great Fen just outside Ely.

It is evening. Two things have happened which Nicodemus could not have known, and I am unsure whether they could have happened together historically, but they appeared together as the nemesis of his life in the novel. What he beholds when he at last gazes out over the marshland, the goal of months of wandering and years of fervent, private communion, is not the wilderness of the sacred marsh but a drainage channel straight as the arrow of God, leading to the horizon and surrounded by regular fields, ditches, dykes and every sign of new agriculture and hydraulic engineering. A Dutch landscape, in effect, humanized, orderly, patiently raised from the fenland broads by the Dutch engineer Vermeyden and now turning the lost Medieval world of the fowlers and fishermen into farmland.

The other thing which Nicodemus could not know about was the iconoclastic destruction of the Lady Chapel in Ely Cathedral, the figures of the Saints and the Evangelists and the Virgin having been smashed and broken and hurled into the waters of the Fen years before. But with the draining of the Fen, the lowering of the waters and the shrinking of the peat beds, on that particular summer evening as Nicodemus falls to his knees at the collapse of his dream, the evening sunlight reveals the broken form of a cathedral statue nearby, half submerged in the mud of a reed-ditch. Nicodemus does not recognize it for a statue, of course, ripped out from the Cathedral. He sees only the figure of Christ, and with this impoverished illusion (the Christ has only one arm and one eye, but Nicodemus does not notice this in his joy) the homely secular landscape of the new engineering is plunged back into a spurious Medieval enchantment. It is a moment of treacherous epiphany, at once plangent and ridiculous, returning the world briefly to the darkening, pathless wastelands of Nicodemus's curious vision.

Set over against this Medieval and extraordinary mystic at the threshold of the New World, with its technical domination of the hidden places of the earth, there was the other half of the novel. This half concerned a modern Vermeyden figure, the modern hydraulics engineer Lucas Arnow working in Sardinia. I have never been to Sardinia. Come to that, it is only since my leukaemia began that I have developed a passionate interest in the 17th century. So I was breaking the first and elementary rule of the novelist—write about what you have experienced and know about. But then, someone inside me *did* know this strange fiction, with its names and settings and narratives. It came from my pen with thoughtless fluency. I felt a mere scribe, a copyist.

The second half of this novel which I scribbled out all through the night those years ago in Norwich has a horrid prescience about it now which hurts me to even think about. Lucas Arnow dies of the malaria which he has come to eradicate. He brings the cure to the local people but dies of the disease in the process. Now malaria isn't leukaemia, but the more I begin to unravel this cathartic fiction of mine from the past, the more connections I feel and understand even if it is too late now. Malaria, leukaemia. My novelistic descriptions of Arnow's physical suffering were entirely fanciful at that time, purely imaginary. But since then I have lived through them all. And now, like him, I am dying of a terrible disease. But it is too late now, of course. Too late altogether.

Lucas Arnow is a professional engineer draining the *stagni*, or foetid coastal marshes in which the malarial mosquitoes breed. For many years I have treasured a quotation from Walter Benjamin which may have helped spawn the character of Arnow or, more likely, contributed something further to a figure already compounded of many memories and unconscious sources:

The slightest carelessness in the digging of a ditch or the buttressing of a dam, the least bit of negligence or selfish behaviour on the part of an individual or group of men in the maintenance of the common hydraulic wealth, becomes, under unusual circumstances, the source of social evils and far-reaching social calamity. Consequently a life-giving river requires on pain of death a close and permanent solidarity.

Lucas Arnow, never having heard of Walter Benjamin, is nevertheless on the side of the common hydraulic wealth. A man of modest and sincere social conscience, a man of *technē*, of the scientific rationalism and practical reason which were so much a part of Fifties optimism and post-war expansion, he works for the common good and with a revulsion against the evils of the marshland—its disease, its mire, its stagnant dangers. He believes strongly in clearing up mess. The foetid pools and malarial reedbeds of the marsh represent, for him, all that civilization has had to struggle against in order to emerge from the primeval slime. It was the humble digger of irrigation channels, the builders of bridges and dams, who first released mankind from inundation, flood and chaos, not Noah. Human life only really began to flourish in the deltas and swamps of the Nile, the Tigris and Euphrates, in Kaneh, in the Holy Land of Cane and Tall Grasses when the mud and filth of the yearly floods were tamed with the measuring rod and the simple shovel. Nothing had really changed, according to Arnow's way of thinking. It was still the sewers and ditches, the reservoirs, waterpipes and dams connected and hidden in one vast, intricate network beneath the earth, which held civilization safe from chaos and disease: the common hydraulic wealth.

I must confess that there was little more to Lucas Arnow than this, and he appears a little small and dry when set beside the fanaticism and inner visionary power of Nicodemus. When I think of Lucas Arnow I see a worthy and anxious man with little humour and even less authority. Even now, by quoting Benjamin and so forth above, I have endowed him with more passion and cosmic vision than he had in the original fiction eleven years ago. Not a particularly attractive person to sustain half a novel—there is something rather abstract and programmatic about him. Indeed, in retrospect, I am astonished at the political symmetry and opposition of these two men, one at the beginning and one at the end (?) of the great arch of bourgeois science and technical control of the world. And what a gulf of time and space I put between Nicodemus the visionary anarchist and Lucas Arnow the progressive rationalist. Three centuries of history and half the length of Europe. This was not a consciously planned or controlled decision, and if I can discover now the links and distance between the two halves of this schizoid fiction then I think I shall have learned something important. Certainly, at the time, the two halves of the novel would not coalesce. They remained obdurately separate and opposed. It was the failure to integrate the two stories satisfactorily into one fiction which eventually prevented me from finishing it. Written in such rhapsodic haste, it just stayed as it was, resistant to any attempt at revision. Its incompleteness has haunted me ever since. Perhaps now, as I go on, I shall be able to finish with it. Finally.

What obsessed me at the time of writing, however, was not Arnow's mind but his death alone. Very little else got sketched in. I called the unfinished novel *Gifts* and it began with Lucas receiving one of the workmen from the marsh into his office. The workman had discovered the rare plant *Erba Sardoa*, the Sardinian herb which, when administered as a poison, produces a horrible rictus upon the face of the victim who is convulsed with 'sardonic' laughter. This 'gift' (in German, this also means *poison*) which opens the novel is a portent of Lucas's end. For he is poisoned, not so much by the malarial swamp, nor even by the interminable delays of machinery and parts which in Fifties Sardinia mimic the stagnation and decay of the marsh itself—though both these natural and institutional evils drain his strength and will. It is really within himself that the poison develops. His entirely laudable but quite limited petit-bourgeois sense of purpose and identity are no match for the miasmic forces welling up inside him. It is precisely the *absence* of magical vision and rage within him, or at least their deep and irrecoverable repression, which cankers his soul. His dykes and dams hold back more than the insidious destructive power of nature:

> Soon, soon, through dykes of our content
> The crumpling flood will force a rent
>   And, taller than a tree,
> Hold sudden death before our eyes
> Whose river dreams long hid the size
>   And vigours of the sea.
>
>   (Auden, 'A Summer Night')

Lucas's death, which terminates his half of the story and which is paralleled by Nicodemus's epiphany on the margin of the Great Fen, was the most intensely-wrought part of the novel. Lucas had been waiting all day for a vital piece of hydraulic equipment (a Bernoulli meter) to arrive from Rome. He is suffering a bad malarial attack, and throughout the long sultry day he drifts in and out of full consciousness, through hallucination, memory and daydream. He becomes superstitiously convinced that his own survival is bound up with the arrival of the Bernoulli meter from Rome. Time and again he asks about it. Towards nightfall he becomes more feverish and ill, and the friend who has been by his bedside in his villa, and his housekeeper, decide that he must be ferried across the bay to the doctor in Muravera (his villa is on a promontory across from the small town, close to the edge of the marsh but also looking out over the sea). The Bernoulli meter has not arrived. As darkness comes, he is carried out to the small fishing boat which also doubles as a local ferry and the boat sets out on the short journey across the bay to the town. Lucas dies before the boat has got half-way across. Strangely, I felt his death in metaphors of communication, a language too modern for Lucas, but that is how it came out:

Lucas was slumped half sitting and half lying in the bottom of the boat. It was warm even out here on the sea. The sky was cloudy and the air thick as if miasmic fingers of bad air had floated out from the marshes onto the surface of the sea in lethargic pursuit of the small boat. Lucas was on his left side with his knees drawn up tight and his hands pushed down between his thighs. A grey blanket was pulled up over his shoulder. He shook his head to clear it and opened his eyes once to look towards the lights of the town. It was useless. His thoughts drifted again. His head began to fill with noises even though the boat was sliding almost silently through the water with only little waveslaps clapping against the bow now and then.

So this was dying. Nothing peaceful about it. Lucas struggled to stay in contact with the boat and the sky and the water but there was that terrible noise. What was it, that crackle and interference which made everything so far away now. Lucas moved his head from side to side very slowly trying to clear his head filled with shapeless and indistinct noises. It was becoming so noisy, so busy. Like a city rush hour. So very noisy and busy. Then there was a final subsidence of all clarity and sharpness into a sea of unfathomable sounds, a voice receding just beyond intelligibility like a radio station fading away in the night. And it was getting louder. Lucas groaned in panic. Something seemed to split and slither deep within his belly. It's not silent not silent at all but loud. There was a rush of pure sound through the air like a wind becoming louder and louder crowding out and pushing through him and over him. A gleeful confusion of bugs and babble tumbled and fell upon him like insects swarming in the darkness. Mosquitoes came, filling up his nose and his mouth until at last his mouth, stuffed with the deafening noises, stiffened into a final rictus of defeat.

But Lucas does hear something just before he dies. Across the empty water of the bay a young boy and his father are fishing from a boat anchored near the shore. The young boy is trailing a line from the stern of the small boat and their voices carry clearly across the surface of the waters. As Lucas dies, there is a sudden disturbance and a splash which Lucas hears like an echo from far off. The last thing that Lucas hears, clearly now, with a preternatural clarity, is the excited voice of the young boy in the darkness. 'Look Papa. Look. Look. A fish. I've caught a fish.'

The Village

Cranfield, the Bedfordshire village in which I was born and grew up, is an unappealing place. From very early on I knew

I disliked it and wanted to get out. Essentially, it is a nonde-
script straggle of houses sandwiched uncomfortably between
the vast London Valley Brickyard in the Marston Valley on
one side, with its hundreds of sulphurous chimneys, and the
airfield on the other side, a leftover from the Second World
War which has since become a college of aeronautics.

When I was a boy, the village reeked of sulphur for much
of the year, whenever the wind blew up the valley from the
brickworks chimneys. The sulphur withered the leaf on the
trees, especially the elms, and it gave me chronic catarrh. I
have a poor sense of smell and blame it on the brickworks.
What perfunctory nasal education I received as a child came
from my visits to my aunt in Grimsby—at least there the
indescribably noxious stink of the Humberside Cod Liver Oil
factory, one whiff of which made me vomit, formed something of a counterpoint with the smell of sulphur. In consequence, my olfactory discrimination as an adult splits the
whole wonderful subtle world of scents and smells into the
codliverish or the sulphurous: reading Proust for the first
time I wept in envy and disbelief.

Despite my innate dislike of Cranfield, it is, like my
leukaemia, in my bones. It is also, in the most oblique and
obdurate way, in my novel, though at first glance the village
could not seem further removed from the 17th-century Fens
and Fifties Sardinia. But weaving backwards and forwards
between childhood memory and recollections of the unfinished fiction, under the duress of my present illness with its
closeness of death, I unearth, here and there, bits of understanding and connectedness. It gives me a luxurious sense of
indulgent self-archaeology. It also helps to keep me alive, like
refusing to die because I haven't heard the end of the story.
My Scheherezade.

Cranfield is geographically not the South, nor the Midlands, nor East Anglia—it sits uncomfortably on a small
plateau between the three areas, pulled in all directions and
blandly unsure of its identity. It is not horribly ugly, which
would at least give it a kind of unlovely value. It is indeterminate and forgetttable, straggly and ad hoc, like so many of

the towns and villages which just fail to be part of the gritty Midlands and also fail to be part of the desolate beauty of East Anglia. Corby, Northampton, Leicester, Kettering—they all appear part of this grey and undistinguished part of the country, and they all give me the same desperate feeling as Cranfield.

There is something lopsided and one-dimensional about the village, caused by the perimeter fence of the airfield which runs its full length and cuts off its northern side. The airfield was built in 1937 and covered Perryfield, Leanfield and Stillipers, a large area which had once been the common land of the village. Undoubtedly the MoD impoverished and diminished the village with its barbed-wire perimeter far more effectively than the centuries of enclosure had managed to do. Naturally the airfield required the flat land for runways and so took most of the small plateau on which the village is built. The result is that Cranfield feels as if it has been shouldered to the very edge of the plateau and is about to slither down Marston Hill into the valley.

So: to the north the barbed-wire perimeter fence of the airfield; to the south the steep slope of the valley ending in the brickworks. There was nowhere to walk to any more. If now you want to wander around, you are forced to parade up the High Street and back, past the numerous new little housing estates which have filled in the spaces where the farms used to be along the village main street: Moat farm, Glebe farm, Washingleys Manor, Orchard Way, Walkhouse. And of course the Old Rectory, a splendid Edwardian monstrosity the decaying and empty rooms of which I used to explore as a boy, has now become a very smart little estate of 'neo-Georgian' houses overlooking the Church. The builders did leave the Cedar tree which used to stand on the Rectory lawn, but it has to be said that it has lost its lordly splendour and seems a trifle embarrassed now, surrounded by a dozen neat neo-Georgian family homes. Too grand and expansive for its surroundings, the cedar is humiliated by its size, an arboreal Gulliver towering above the Lilliputian privet and suburban forsythia.

When I was a young boy, however, this rather spiritless village had one wonderful compensation. Have you noticed that children, wherever they can, make their own secret pathways and tracks around their neighbourhood by following ditches and waterways, often inaccessible to adults? Water-pipes with nasty spiked collars at each end, stretched across rivers, often prove more popular crossing-points for children, especially gangs of young boys, than the bridge down the road. Ditches, streams, ponds and pools, culverts under the dual-carriageway or the railway line—these places form a semi-secret network of tracks, hiding-places and dens which adults half-notice but never see in the way children do.

Cranfield had a rich hinterland of such waterways, particularly old moats and ponds, running through fields and back-gardens the whole length of the village. They were alternative, secret byways for the children of the village. Adults rarely strayed there, yet especially during the school holidays the hedges and ponds and ditches were alive with children. This was my world. I seem to have spent much of my childhood playing around these places, trekking from one to the other, building secret camps in the willows, constructing dams and bridges, catching newts, tadpoles and sticklebacks, venturing out onto the ice in winter. One time we built a raft from old oil-drums, and, too afraid to sail on it ourselves, we tethered one of David Luck's hapless chickens to its deck and sent it on a squawking unhappy journey downstream. Another time we constructed an elaborate camp on a small island in the middle of a pond with a rope drawbridge worked by discarded bell-ropes from the Church.

I only learned recently that Cranfield has a unique local history in respect of the moats and ditches which were strung along its length. There were dozens of them and the local archivist remarks in his history of the village that 'numerous ponds have long been a common feature of the Cranfield landscape'. In addition to the many natural ponds there are the curious Cranfield moats dating from the 12th and 13th centuries. Evidently most of the farmsteads in the parish were moated or rebuilt within their moats as late as the 19th century and show a remarkable historical continuity from Medieval times. Wood End, Moat farm, East End farm, Boxhedge House, Eyreswood farm, Broad Green farm, Perry Hill farm—all had moats, and some of these remained up to a few years ago. The Parish Survey records in 1722 the 'Messuage in Cranfield built by Dr William Aspin, with the moat round it and groves of trees adjoining'. There is no clear explanation for the existence or indeed the survival of these moats, since no other local parishes appear to have them. Moat farm was still completely encircled with water when I was a boy, and almost every old house in the village had a pond or part of a moat somewhere nearby. As children, we could make our way clear from one end of the village to the other by trailing from one pond to another, and they were often connected up with ditches and drainage channels. Our own house, dating from the 1800s, had a curious bridge built into one side-wall, spanning a marshy piece of land, probably too boggy to support the foundations.

It is only now and in the light of my old novel that I see how my childhood imagination was formed in close and unconscious connection with the odd, moated history of my village.

Its abandoned moats and watercourses were a secret domain which filled my days. Concealed by copses of willow, bullrushes and overgrown hedgerow, there was a magical calm and concealment about this marshy realm. There was also something melancholic and a little frightening, too, since the water never flowed. All these ponds and moats were green and stagnant, as still as death. They had long since clogged with weed and flotsam, the drainage pipes smashed and the interconnecting ditch dammed up here and there with mud and undergrowth. And the ponds were a common dumping-ground for village refuse: piles of old bricks, rusting bicycles, even one or two old cars. Whatever their original purpose, as the years went by these moats and ponds were filled-in and built-over. So in one sense it is clear that Nicodemus, on his slow pilgrimage from the Midlands to the

Fens, was in search not only of God and the reeds, but of my own vanished childhood.

As time went on these ponds and pools which so fascinated me as a boy disappeared one by one. The moat system which had lasted from Medieval times to the 1950s was buried in less than ten years, first under rubble and landfill, then under new housing and tarmac. Each summer holiday there were fewer and fewer ponds and pools. I felt very sorry for the frogs and the newts crushed beneath the tons of broken brick and earth. These trivial deaths really bothered me. Only a few years ago I wrote a strange and not very good poem about a poor frog, again, at the time, unaware of the origins of my concern. God how the gloomy enchantment of those stagnant places held me in thrall. Yet it was only four years ago, at the age of 32, that I began to learn *why* these marshy moats and stygian pools have exerted such an exorbitant grip upon my unconscious throughout my life.

I came to learn that the most important single event of my childhood was the death of my young sister, Carol. Without the least suspicion, I had lived, worked and loved in the shadow of her death. Its hold upon me had been as complete as it was unsuspected. Certainly, when I wrote the novel my drowned sister never entered my head. But all those marshes and swamps, the Great Fen and the Sardinian *stagni*, Nicodemus saved and Lucas Arnow dead, how clearly now they seem displacements of my childhood mourning and terror, my obsessive lingering at the pool's edge summer and winter all the years of my growing up. But I did not know it then, I thought it was about other things—which it also was, as I shall describe in due course. But I know that the death of my sister Carol was the secret kernel to my marshland fiction.

For it was in one of these village ponds that Carol drowned. It was 1956, and I was five years old. Carol and her twin sister Debbie were three. It was summertime and very hot. Carol simply wandered off down the overgrown garden and squeezed through a hole in the hedge, disappearing within seconds. Her body was recovered the next day when they dragged the pond. The pond had been covered in

Canadian pond weed from edge to edge and looked just like a beautifully smooth lawn. She probably walked, or ran, straight into it, thinking it was a garden.

A Screen Memory

I was playing on the back lawn. It was a really hot July afternoon and I was five years old. There was a small sand heap on one corner of the grass not far from the garden swing and the old plum tree. I was a bit bored and listless. I had a white sunhat on and I was idly shovelling sand with a small tin seaside spade, red with a wooden handle. Carol was a bit further down the lawn away from the house. Gradually she began to wander down the garden further and further away from the house and away from me. I knew that she shouldn't go that far down the lawn, and I knew that she would get into trouble, but I didn't say anything. I just watched without speaking, a small boy motionless and silent, no longer digging, but watching his little sister waddling off down the garden into the long grass. I watched until she had disappeared. I knew that she was doing something bad and that she might be hurt or become lost. But I stayed quite still and silent, calling neither to my mother nor to Carol. This memory, carrying with it the full burden of guilt for my sister's death, I experienced with unbearable clarity. I was responsible. I could have stopped her. I knew she was going to lose herself in the perilous forbidden places at the bottom of the garden, but I said nothing. I wanted her dead. I hated her. So I stood silently in the sunshine, five years old, making one or two idle marks on the sand with my seaside spade, watching her go.

This memory, etched into my mind with the clarity of total recall, is false. I was not in the garden at the time when she wandered off. According to my mother, I was elsewhere, playing with a friend in his garden. I couldn't have seen her go. It was impossible. I was not there.

The Realm of Estrangement

Since I contracted leukaemia my father and I have been much closer. There is no chance now of being unfinished with one another. He has held me to him. He cares for me. And after a fashion, we talk to one another about important things. Believe me, it hasn't always been like that. Like so many of my friends, I have spent most of my life feeling estranged from my parents in some vague and indefinite way. And the old clichés about lack of communication and parents just not understanding and children not caring all seemed justified. Up until my illness I felt more and more alarmed that as my parents got older they would die before we had said how much we cared for each other, before we forgave each other. I wanted family closeness and for us all to talk openly to each other. Of course it never quite entered my head that it was not my parents who would die, but me.

It is impossible to say whether my illness is connected with the death of my sister all those years ago. Perhaps, as I sometimes think, it is pure biological malignancy quite unrelated to my spiritual life, a random incident at the level of genetic material and swarming cells as far removed from my unconscious and my history as some galaxy remote in the heavens. Yet the prescience of my fiction disturbs me. Malaria. Leukaemia. Disease of the blood. A life which, at every crisis, turned broodingly to images of shady ponds and stagnant waters, death by drowning. I remember one afternoon not too long after Carol's death when I was wandering aimlessly around the old greenhouse at the bottom of the garden. Again it was a hot summer's day. At the back of the greenhouse there was a waterbutt filled to the brim. I could only just see over the edge. Waterlilies floated silently on the warm still water. It was preternaturally quiet, the day held in suspension by the heat and stillness. I was quite alone and I stood on tiptoe grasping the edge of the rusted butt staring at the water's reflective surface of thick green liquid. Movement came only from one or two mayflies skating back and forth between the lilies. I seem to be held there for ever, even now, peering into the depths of the water, trying to get down beneath the surface, amongst the coiled stems of the lilies and the shoals of tiny white wireworms wriggling and disappearing into the green depths.

In the early days of my leukaemia two years ago I was convinced that this death wish, this identification with my drowned sister, was responsible for my illness. Three things, tangled up together but separate, seemed involved. The first was identification: inside me somewhere Carol actually constituted a part of my being, she was me. Not as a part of my personality, but as something much more physical, an hysterical body, a violence which terrifies me even when expressed as mere words here on the page. I can hardly begin to approach this level of my being: Here Be Monsters. Nothing can be held steady enough for language in this place, things flicker and slide, shapes loom and melt away. There is none of that elegiac lyricism of drowning and summer afternoons here—gentle *kaddish* for the dead. Here it burns and hurts. It is violent, spasmodic, monstrous. There is no wholeness. I am not *myself* here. I can bear to stay here no longer.

But there is a second thing, a second way in which Carol's death is inside me—less exorbitant, a little more approachable, perhaps. I took upon myself, at the age of five, complete and sole responsibility for her death. It hardly matters that in fact so did everyone else in the family, each one of us taking up the burden alone, never dreaming that we had all done the same. Nor did it matter that I didn't 'understand' death at that age. I understood enough to know that a terrible crime had taken place. There were policemen standing awkwardly in the kitchen, anguished tears from my mother carried sobbing round to Grandma's house, whispers, knots of people gathered outside the house, groups of men from the village coming and going throughout the day late into the night. How a child takes on the guilt of death and separation I don't know, but before the body had been found something inside me had already decided that I was responsible for the crime, that I had a dreadful guilty secret that I would henceforth carry with me unknown to myself for thirty years. And like the sense of seduction in Freud, the truth or falsehood of the matter was utterly irrelevant.

The third element in Carol's death was the childhood puzzle of death itself and my unresolved mourning for her sudden, permanent disappearance. I did not attend the funeral and until last year she remained somehow unburied for me. I could not 'put her away', too many unfinished and importuning emotions remained.

The fact of my leukaemia intervened across all this with an extraordinary new possibility of resolution. After some months of acute illness it became clear that the only thing which might save my life was a bone-marrow transplant. This still remains the major hope of cure for most people with the disease. Sadly, it requires a closely matched donor for the marrow, and by far the most important group of donors are siblings—the brothers and sisters of the victim. The chances of a sibling possessing a suitable marrow are about four to one. This means that, taken with those patients who have no siblings, less than 15 per cent of leukaemia sufferers will have a marrow-donor.

There seemed something marvellously providential when we discovered that my sister Debbie was a perfect match. A real prospect of cure was suddenly available. My sister would save me. She was delighted. She was proud and happy to be able to help fight for my life. Always somewhat distant from each other in the past, we were suddenly brought really close. We laughed at the curious fact that the transplant would change my blood-group to hers, that we should indeed become blood relatives.

Remember that Debbie was Carol's twin sister. They were identical. Gradually the symbolic force of it all began to dawn on me. The marrow of twins is perfectly matched. If, somehow, my morbid identification with Carol were in some complicated way connected to my falling ill, then how perfect that her marrow, her blood, in Debbie, should be used to save my life. It could not fail. I felt no religious redemption involved, but the poetic logic of it was overwhelming. I felt joyful and confident that such a pattern had emerged. It just seemed impossible that it would not work. Debbie would give me life just as Carol had threatened to take my life away. Carol had made me ill, Debbie would make me well again.

I passed the summer months before the transplant in a largely confident and happy mood. I set about trying to settle the account with Carol. I needed to rid myself of all that stagnant water and muddy morbidity, shake it off once and for all. I needed to be able to bury her at last, peacefully and permanently. I needed to let go of her. I went to a therapist and worked through all that I have told you and I slowly and carefully tried to find good ways of ending her mournful tyranny over my life.

When the twins were born, my father had planted two lovely juniper trees either side of the path in the garden. Tiny saplings, they had been intended to grow with the twins as they grew up. When Carol died, either my father deliberately dug up one of the trees or it died: in any case, only one tree was left. Debbie's tree, after Carol's death. It remained on the left-hand side of the pathway guarding the way down to the bottom of the garden and the orchard. In one of my therapeutic sessions I had a clear and purposeful vision of Debbie's tree, now very tall and straight, over thirty years old, and I knew that it symbolized life and hope for me. I also knew that I should replant Carol's tree, a new tree in the position of the old one, and that this, too, would give me life and strength. I also felt that, at last, I should be able to symbolically bury Carol for myself in the planting of this tree. And it was not enough merely to have this vision. I must actually do it, actually buy a juniper sapling and go back to the old house and plant it as it had been.

My brother-in-law thought I was crazy, Debbie said she understood but had her doubts, my parents seemed to think that anything which helped was all right. So I planted the tree. I dug the hole in the earth, but before I put the tree into it I placed a small wooden box beneath the roots with a rose inside it and a short prayer to Carol asking her to help me. The tree looked beautiful. Shortly afterwards I went into hospital and had the transplant, which seemed a great success. For six months I grew strong again until the following May when, suddenly, I relapsed. The leukaemia was back. The transplant had failed.

Great-Grandma and the Well

The Whites have lived in Cranfield for at least two hundred years and for most of that time the men of the family were village artisans and craftsmen. The family business seems to have covered a variety of skilled trades, but for most of the 19th century the Whites were gunsmiths and watchmakers. By the turn of the century my great-grandfather was also running the local post and telegraph office as well as selling and repairing bicycles, making and repairing guns, clocks and watches. Omnicompetent, occupying sprawling premises in the centre of the village, by the time of the Great War the Whites were a village institution, one step down in importance from the Vicar and one step up from the local farmers and other tradesfolk. However, when my great-grandfather died, my great-grandma did a curious thing. She took all the guns and clocks which he had in his workshop, all the spare parts and bits of mechanism which he had needed for his trade, and she threw them down the well in the back yard. From that moment on, the family gunsmithing and watch-mending were at an end.

It gives me a most peculiar feeling to imagine that moment when the guns and clocks, pendulums, cogs, and tiny fragments of mechanism, were hurled into the well. They must all have rusted to nothing by now deep beneath the back-garden. My father says that great-grandma did it because she was afraid of the guns in the house, but that doesn't account for the clocks and the bits and pieces. She certainly didn't want her son following his father's trade, that's for sure. From that time on, the post office and a heavier kind of engineering—agricultural vehicles and such—became the mainstay of the family.

Indeed, the skills and abilities of the Whites closely followed the technical and engineering developments of the century: from guns and clocks to bicycles and early farm machinery in my great-grandfather's time, through to lorries and finally cars in my father's time. By the time I was born

'Allon White & Son' had been moving quietly with—or just behind—the times since before the First World War and was a small but modestly successful village garage. A quiet local business, it was as ready to mend bicycle punctures and pull farm tractors out of ditches as it was to sell Morris cars, repair lorries and taxi Mrs Malsher to hospital on the third Thursday of every month. The post office and the garage were run side by side. Between the wars great-aunt Tess used to run the village telephone switchboard where each phone had a jack-plug of its own and the operator listened in and personally relayed every call (there is a splendid and hilarious example in the Ealing comedy *Whisky Galore*). Every Saturday morning great-grandfather used to open the back parlour as a barber's shop. He bought a special barber's chair with a high back and neck-rest which swung down for shaving, and each week men from the village would gather round the back of the house for a haircut, a shave and a gossip. I don't know exactly when the Whites ceased to be village barbers—probably on the death of great-grandfather along with the gun and clock repairs, I suspect. The post office and the garage became more and more important over the years. Practical, hard-working, unpretentious, without wide ambitions, the men of the family from great-grandfather down to my own father carried the business on generation after generation.

A certain timidity and caution marked these men despite their innovations and diversity of skills. They kept out of controversy just as they seem to have kept out of the pubs (of which there were at least nine in Cranfield in great-grand-father's time). The family had some status in the community and was well respected, partly because of the very centrality and diversity of its functions, partly because of a reputation for scrupulousness and fair dealing, and partly because of its long history in Cranfield. Despite a near hegemonic monopoly on every village activity—post and telegraph, barbering, agricultural machinery and blacksmithing, taxi and car repairs, guns, clocks and watches—the men had an unassuming and down-to-earth quality which well suited local people.

I think the women of the family have always been somewhat more ambitious and class-conscious than their husbands. In part, this is because they have come into the village from outside—and my mother's story is an extreme case of this which I shall come to presently. But grandfather married a bit above himself when he courted my grandma—at least so she was fond of hinting to me as a child, and indeed she was of gentry stock and introduced a new level of social accomplishment into the family. She had studied music in Paris, spoke some French, played the piano extremely well and tirelessly corrected the rustic manners of her husband, children and grandchildren. In the Thirties grandfather briefly became the owner of a Rolls-Royce, which he hired out for all the local weddings and used as a taxi to ferry local people to Bedford on market day. In the Fifties my father's sister married the Vicar's son and a little later the other sister married an Air Force officer: grandfather was chairman of the Harter Trust which administered the almshouses.

My great-grandfather was called Allon White and I am named after him. The family firm has been called Allon White & Son since just after the Great War—indeed I have a photograph taken in 1920 of the post office and bicycle shop with 'Allon White & Son' displayed boldly across the front. This shop sign tells two stories, one about the distant family past and one about myself.

The first story is just a speculation of mine and there is no one left alive to confirm it or deny it. However, I possess an even earlier photograph than the one I have mentioned. This earlier photograph was taken around 1910 or 1912 and the whole family stands informally in the garden in front of the post office: great-grandfather with his full-length white apron, my grandfather aged about twelve sitting on the fence beside his brother Alwyn, aged about fourteen; great-grandma in a full-sleeved silk blouse and her two daughters; finally the two village postmen in their uniforms holding their bicycles, with Tinker the dog sitting alert and watchful in one of the front baskets. Between the two photographs the First World War intervened. Uncle Alwyn, grandad's elder brother (14 years old in the picture), was called up for active service and contracted TB in the trenches. He was invalided home and, since it was thought that fresh air was helpful for TB, lived and slept either in the wash-house or in a tent in the back garden throughout the winter. He died in 1919. Since my grandfather was two years younger than Alwyn he only got called up at the end of the war (he always maintained that he was the last man in England to go into the Royal Flying Corps—the day following his enlistment it became the Royal Air Force). The second photograph was taken about a year later, about 1920, and whereas the shop sign before the war read simply 'Allon White', the sign after the war has added '& Son'. There was only one son left now, my grandfather, and he is taken up onto the shop sign very shortly after Alwyn's death—in defiance, or pride, or compensation, who knows: 'Allon White & Son'.

The second story concerns me. My name is Allon White. Throughout my childhood and growing up it was *my* name on the sign over the garage and over the post office, on the letter-heads and the envelopes. From long before my birth I was enchained in that *Allon White & Son* as thoroughly as young Paul in *Dombey & Son*. It was as if both the past and the future were already firmly in place, me to replace grandfather, my son to replace me in an endless, pre-ordained chain of signifiers. My prescribed destiny seemed written up on the housefront for all to see. How cruelly, how closely the convention of '. . . & Son' can bind business and genealogy together: the old family firm. If you had wondered where all those engineers were coming from in the novel, it should now be apparent. Lucas Arnow the hydraulics engineer was in part the man I should have been had I not broken with my own 'proper' name. The novel was not simply about my attempts to escape from Carol and the miasma of marshland and drowning. It was also about my breaking away from a pre-ordained class and family history, which in my case meant ending that history since I was the only son, the final son, and the history carried my name. In retrospect, I see that this wrench away from my ascribed place in the chain of names was both more protracted and traumatic than I realized at the time. But this came gradually. At first it did not weigh upon me.

The Garage

As a boy I loved the garage. It was a magical place. The English, unlike the Americans and the Italians, have never understood the romance of the garage. To understand what 'Allon White & Son's' garage looked and felt like when I was a young boy in the Fifties you have to go to Italian or American films—to that dusty village garage in Visconti's *Ossessione*, with its one tall petrol-pump and piles of old tyres and rusty parts and a lorry jacked up waiting to be repaired. Or you have to go to those lonely gas stations in the Midwest of the Hollywood 'road' films, miles from anywhere, with a line of telegraph posts disappearing across an empty plain to the horizon. Of course I'm romancing a bit, but garages have changed so much since the Fifties that they have become completely transformed and it is hard to imagine what they were like just after the Second War. Now they tend to be full of *new* things: brightly-coloured pieces of machines, lifts, Krypton testers, the noise of high-technology machinery competing with transistor radios. They have to be *busy* now, and rather colourful like shops (they become more and more like little supermarkets every day, or they perish).

Colour and pace are relatively recent in garage life. The garage of my boyhood was like a wonderful, quiet museum. Everything was old. There were two large workshops, several store-rooms, attics, a few sheds and an office. The whole premises were crammed with parts and tools and spares going back decades, much of it completely out of date. Valve radios, blacksmithing equipment, anvils, even bits of old tack and harness. Boxes and boxes of curious 'things' stored everywhere, of no conceivable use any longer but never cleared out. The place was a secret store of fascinating, inexplicable bits and pieces to play with. Old engines and gearboxes were stored in the pigsty. An orchard surrounded the workyard at the back and lorries sometimes broke branches of blossom from the apple trees as they were wheeled in for repair.

Even with four or five mechanics working there it was usually peaceful with only occasional bouts of rhythmic hammering or the revving of a motor. There was an old red air-compressor in the corner of one workshop and it was switched on at eight every morning. It had an uncannily human bronchial condition and began each day uncertainly with an impersonation of chronic whooping-cough. For the rest of the time it intruded rather quietly on the day and then only at long intervals. The pace was very, very slow. Each mechanic usually worked alone, and so for most of the time, absorbed in separate tasks under cars or lorries, rarely spoke. My father and grandfather, as well as two uncles, worked alongside the other mechanics in their oily overalls, and I suppose it was because they were there that I was allowed to spend so much time in the workshops even as a small child. An old brown bakelite radio played away, apparently to itself, in one corner of the main workshop every day.

I remember my father's dirty, oily hands. They are calloused and cracked, with the grime deep black in the cuts and grazes round his knuckles. His hands are so large and dirty. I am very small. They are rough and smelly when he touches me. I don't want hands like that. I never want hands like that. Dirty and oily. He puts his fingers into a Dundee marmalade pot which he keeps on the kitchen window sill. It is full of a slimy red oil-jelly to clean off his dirty hands before lunch. The oil-jelly smells of paraffin. His hands have black cracks all over the palms.

Nevertheless I am gradually drawn into the world of the workshop. Little by little, imperceptibly moving from play to errands and small tasks and then to work. At first I squatted beside a car or sat on the anvil and played with welding-rods or a huge box of old motorbike spokes stored in the corner. The petrol pump attendant was a young woman called Janet and she used to look after me. On sunny days I could play with my matchbox toys on the dusty forecourt between the petrol pumps. So few cars called for petrol in those days that I could trace out elaborate roadways in the gravel and play all morning there without having to move out of the way for customers. Most days I returned home covered in oil. I can remember one summer day when I was sitting on the kerb in front of the garage so covered in grease and dirt that all the village women who went past laughed and told me that I'd be for it when my mother saw me.

Sometimes the garage frightens me. Horace Riddy is trying to lever a punctured tractor tyre from its rim. The rear wheel of the tractor, orange and covered in mud, is huge and takes three men to wheel into the workshop before they let it roll forwards on its own to crash down on the floor. I like Horace. He stands on the wheel and drives a great steel ram again and again into the edge of the tyre to break the seal. I put my hands over my ears but he continues, smashing the ram against the steel rim. It is winter, and his breath hangs white in the air. There is ice round the hub bolts. Horace has skinned the flesh from his hand with the ram, but he continues to pound at the unrelenting tyre.

As I got older, I began to run small errands for the mechanics. Their morning tea-break was at ten and they used to send me down to Sampson's grocery to buy them fruit pies: Lyons fruit pies at sixpence each. These pies came with a bewildering number of different fillings and the mechanics were very particular about this, specifying and listing with great care who was to have which filling—apple and blackberry for Sam, apricot for Ken, blackcurrant for Paul, and so on. Time and again they would make out the list and slip in a request for some quite impossible fruit filling which they had concocted, warning me that I really mustn't get it wrong. Off I would trot down to the shop clutching a handful of sixpences in one hand and diligently running through the list in my head. 'And Sam wants a plum and marmalade pie,' I would say to the shoplady, who was in on the conspiracy. 'Well, we're out of those love, but why don't you just run back up to the garitch and tell him we've got a fresh batch of damson and peanut—lovely they are.' So back up the High Street I would run, perhaps half a dozen times, willing and completely unsuspecting, chasing imaginary fruit pies with impossible fillings throughout the day—a fruitless task.

The same thing happened with errands to the spares department. It didn't take me long to cotton on to dire warnings that the screws *had* to be 'left-handed and headless half-inchers'. But I spent many an hour scouring the shelves for a 'Vauxhall Vicar's Rubber Gaiter (screw thread only)' or some other such marvellous spare part.

The mechanics increasingly adopted this playful and teasing attitude towards me as I became more involved with serious jobs in the workshop. In some ways it was the beginning of my political education. I was the boss's son, bright, innocent, and definitely not one of the workshop mechanics however much I tried to please. None of them was ever cruel, and indeed often they were friendly and generous, but there was at bottom a mistrust which I could never appease. I was compromised. They sometimes let me know, with a broad wink, that they were 'borrowing' a gallon of oil or some tool or other for home. They knew that I wouldn't betray the theft and they also knew it made me feel awkward and ashamed. They took advantage of my youth to revenge themselves upon my grandfather, father and the firm itself. At dinnertime my dad would sadly and bitterly recount how this or that was missing, how he knew that someone was thieving. I felt his hurt and hated the theft but sat silently, unable to betray the men for whom I was now a kind of occasional apprentice.

Ken

Ken had pale, slate-grey eyes and his forehead sloped back severely so that when he stared at you it looked as if his head were thrown back in contemptuous laughter. His teasing was more violent than the others' and yet he fascinated me. He taught me dirty. 'Go and tell your mother to "fuck off",' he would whisper to me, winking at the other mechanics (did I? I don't remember). He put on little acts of deliberate vulgarity: excavated his huge nose with his oily fingers crooked like crow's feet, his strange pale eyes rolling and his teeth gritted in a manic grin. He could fart prodigiously and at will—sometimes it was his only contribution to a conversation and invariably the last word. Sometimes if I asked him for something he would look at me slyly and give a long, thin fart as his only reply. He would drink Tizer and belch magnificently. I could do neither. His scornful play lives with me still: he suddenly arches forward and ambles towards me, rounding his shoulders and dropping his knuckles to the floor, neanderthal now, grunting and staring, cigarette smoke billowing from his nostrils as he chases me shrieking round the workshop. He taught me to swear and I still do—his sinister, hilarious lessons in fuckpissshit have become an unstable, eruptive substratum to my cultured university language. He used the grotesque and the lower body and dirty orifices and taught me all the Bakhtin I know.

Welding

My father said, 'I can weld spiders' webs,' and I believed him. No one could weld like my father. I loved working late in the darkened workshop beside him, holding a clamped piece of metal or a lamp. At the core of the oxy-acetylene flame there was a tiny cat's tongue of liquid silver which had to lick the metal. It was the hottest part of the torch, sheathed both by a violet spear and an outer orange plume of flame. My father would slowly play the different colours of the flame against the metal until suddenly it would sigh and fuse with itself, the crack gone, the gap filled. I often stood by his side watching him do this, filled with excitement and envy. Perhaps there was also a kind of oedipal longing, for welding was a man's job in the garage and learning to weld was a rite of passage—one which I never accomplished. And I really regret that I never learned to weld: it remains for me a kind of alchemy mixing the magic of the workshop with childhood time with my father. It might even have made a man of me. But by the time I was old enough and strong enough to wheel about the huge gas cylinders of oxygen and acetylene I had already begun to lose interest in the garage.

The Bernoulli Meter

I have been reflecting on that piece of equipment—the Bernoulli meter—which Lucas Arnow was waiting for in the novel. It flickers in and out of his consciousness during the long day of malarial fever and becomes a sort of talisman or fetish, connected in his mind with his own illness. If the meter arrives then he will live. By the early evening the fever clears a little and he wakes to find his friend Fabrizio beside his bed:

Lucas awoke suddenly. The flood had subsided within him and the swelling of his upper arms and mouth seemed to have gone. He rubbed his hand across his forehead and felt the drying salt of his sweat sticky against his palm. He felt thirst, but calm at last. He could move his head. Fabrizio still sat beside the bed in the twilight waiting for the return of Marietta with the doctor. As the light faded, the mosquitoes on the marsh rose up in silent clouds to greet the darkness and began softly to invade the margins of the shore. Fabrizio flicked down the netting around Lucas's bed and sat back, shifting his weight in the wicker chair which creaked once.

—Fabrizio?

—Yes Lucas.

—The fever has left me. Now I am alone.

—You're not alone Lucas, I am here, over here, look at me. Marietta is fetching the doctor. You are all right.

Lucas turned towards his friend and attempted to raise himself on his elbow but his arm would not move properly. He did not smile.

—But I am alone Fabrizio.

Fabrizio did not know what to say. There was a long silence. The mosquito netting shivered and shifted silently with the last exhalation of the day.

—Yes Lucas, you are alone.

—And the Bernoulli meter did not come?

The rate of flow will not be determined, the valve will not be connected and the measurements will not take place. Bernoulli's theorem, upon which the simple and highly efficient measuring device of the meter is constructed, will not, here on the coast of Sardinia, find its place in the hydrometric control of the world. Stagni stagni stagni. Let them die. Lucas turned back to stare across the dark bay. Fabrizio leant forward and covered his shoulder with the sheet patched damp from the fever.

—No the Bernoulli meter did not come, Lucas.

What disappointment of desire, beyond mere superstition, is imagined in that Bernoulli meter? It is precisely a measuring device, the measure of all desire, inflated by Lucas's desperation into a symbol to ward off not only his death but the entropic degeneration of the earth. But that's not the half of it. In reflecting on the novel so closely over these last days I have discovered an over-intensity of connectedness to the Bernoulli meter which astonishes me. Of course it shouldn't surprise me at all: for years I have taught my students about Freud's theory of condensation, in which every symbol condenses within it not one but a number of different contents. It has an unconscious economy which brings different desires or fears into one concentrated image. And so indeed it proves with the meter.

The science of hydraulics was born in 1738, when Daniel Bernoulli published his *Hydrodynamica*. The Bernoulli meter as such does not exist, and at first I called it a Venturi meter, which was invented in 1887 by an American, Clement Herschel, for measuring the flow of liquids and was named in honour of the Italian scientist Venturi. The Venturi meter depends upon Bernoulli's theorem for its operation, and I changed the name from Venturi to Bernoulli to celebrate and retain the symbolic history of hydromechanics from its origin. It is interesting in view of what follows that both names signify a certain 'Italianness', which is relevant to my story.

What was the Bernoulli meter doing in the novel? Last week it suddenly occurred to me as so obvious that it made me laugh out loud. Throughout my youth I had listened, day after day, to a single lament from my father: why hadn't the —— arrived from Bedford yet? The —— was some spare

part or other needed for the completion of a job in the
garage, a carburettor cable or a clutch plate or a tyre or
valve spring or something without which the job remained
unfinished. Day in, day out, lunchtimes and teatimes, my
father would ritually butter his bread whilst intoning his
litany of frustrations, this job held up, that job pushed aside,
because the distributors hadn't delivered such-and-such a
spare part. Or, as happened with unbelievable frequency,
they had delivered the wrong part (sometimes three or four
times) which had to be returned costing yet more delay. The
customers complained and got angry, jobs drifted on for
days, sometimes weeks, and my father drifted into migraine
and depression.

So, the Bernoulli meter was the condensation of a thou-
sand spare parts spread over a decade and a half which had
worn my father down with their delays and confusions. Its
very triviality as a small measuring device was significant.
Trapped between the large distributors and irate, impatient
customers, my father suffered acutely from these minor tra-
vails. A quiet and gentle man, he hated 'scenes', and whenever there was a delay he could sense impending trouble and
shrank back. Like so many men worried at work, he brought
his anxiety back to the privacy of the family dinner table and
turned it into a set narrative, automatic after a while, which
I must have heard hundreds of times. It confirmed me in my
hardening decision that I would never work as he had done,
that I would never suffer the same helplessness and frustra-
tion, that I would never work in the garage. This became
obvious to both of us as I entered my teens and he began to
look around for other people who might take my place in
Allon White & Son.

The finest mechanics by far whom my father had
employed were two Italian brothers, Giuseppi ('Jo') and
Louis. After the war thousands of Italians had been brought
into Bedford and the surrounding area on work contracts at
the brickworks. They had to work for about four years and
then, if they wished, they could take other jobs. Most of
these Italians came from the Mezzogiorno around Naples

and stayed on—Bedford has the highest number of Italian immigrants in the country and even has an Italian consulate. I grew up with the second generation of the original migrant workers and Jo and his brother were a few years older than I was. At school several of my friends were second generation Italian and by the Sixties Bedford had a thriving Italian sub-culture.

Jo in particular was an outstanding mechanic. He started work in the garage when he was about seventeen and quickly proved to be a better mechanic than Sam the foreman. After some years he was ready to set up a workshop on his own but lacked the capital. Meanwhile my father was becoming more and more convinced that I wasn't going to join the firm and began to think that he would take Jo into partnership, which he finally did in 1965. Jo effectively became my substitute, my replacement, and I felt a mixture of guilt and relief at the arrangement.

At first the idea worked well. Jo was able to persuade many Italians from Bedford to make the ten-mile journey out to Cranfield to have work done on their cars, and so the number of customers at the garage grew. Jo became foreman/manager and my father largely ceased manual work in the garage and took to his office to run the expanding business.

One day my father came down from his office to discover six large cases of Chianti in the middle of the workshop. For some months the accounts had been going awry and the Chianti was the first ominous sign that another mode of exchange than the official one might be taking place. 'Non ti preoccupare, Eric' smiled Jo with an airy wave of his hand, 'Don't worry about it. It's from Roberto, for the worka we done on the Jaguar.' My father did worry about it. As the weeks went by, two separate and competing economies grew up in the garage side by side, one rooted in the exchange-and-favour system of Southern Italy, the other rooted in the scrupulous petit-bourgeois accountancy of the English Protestant ethic. The accounts were chaotic. Half of the work passing through the garage now had no paperwork to it at all: Jo kept a note of it in his head to exchange against present or future 'favours'. We started eating Italian bread. Strange Italians would arrive unexpectedly to do plumbing jobs or mend the fence. Hundreds of tins of tomato puree would suddenly appear from nowhere.

I think the crisis finally came during the wine-making season. By the late Sixties the Italian community in Bedford was importing lorryloads of grapes from family back in Southern Italy so that they could produce their own wine locally— which they did, in abundance. That year it seemed as thought most of it ended up stacked in the workshop of Allon White & Son in payment for services rendered. We had our own wine lake. My father was in despair. Money— real money—had dwindled to almost nothing despite the large increase in trade. The garage began to resemble a customs warehouse at Villafranchia or Torino, full of unidentifiable and perishable Italian foods. 'Mozzarella,' my father would moan into his dinner plate at night. 'We haven't got any,' replied mother. 'Haven't we though,' said my father. 'Haven't we though.'

The partnership was dissolved amicably and Jo went back to Naples to set up his own garage there. He returned to Bedford a few years later having been driven out of Italy, so he said, by violent demands and extortion. 'Perhaps the mozzarella was a blessing,' murmured my father.

2 Why Am I a Literary Critic?

I am aware that this, for me, is dangerous. It is all a matter of distance. Always I am underdistanced, too close to memory, too close to my past. When I write therefore I write with the hand and the eye of my other to guide me and keep me safe. Between my memories and my eye place the pillow and the sweating (now now, I feel the gorge rise, the sob in the throat). How *close* now, how perilous the thing must be, the stamping of the beast upon the shore. I am a critic because there in the writing out of the other the distance is perfect and I am safe. There are only the minor ecstasies of a triumphant intellect and an inverted image, a virtual 'I'. Yet, and yet. For some reason as I approach the age of three and thirty something is coming closer and closer to me out of my own past and I know that I shall be a literary critic for very little longer. All year I have written, intensely, of hysteria. Hysteria and Francis Bacon (OH! how I understand those awful paintings!): hysteria and carnival: hysteria and modernism. Of course this tide of fear and sadness is my own and soon I know that it will be merely *hysteria*—a small thing, but mine own. What is it then that insists on visiting me? If it were only in the dark, alone (as I guess it always has been, one way or another, all my dreamlong youth) then I could perhaps keep it away for a little while yet. But it comes to me now when I am with others, in the classroom teaching *The Waves*, or at dinnerparties when there is a sudden lull in the talk. It becomes audacious. Look! I am rocking back and forth at the desk as I type like a child in pain. I know that it is there at the fingersends, lurking amongst the keys, waiting for the right combination of letters to release it howling out at me, free at last. Oh memories, what are you that I have kept you there so long? Why do I perspire and

Previously unpublished; written c.1984.

rock in my chair? Why do I breathe so shallowly as though I were afraid to wake you up? Why now after thirty years do you come back to frighten me, a grown man respectable in the accomplishments of his craft? If only I could stop rocking back and forth! This is crazy! (Look how I overdistance again, using my selfconsciousness as a protection against myself.) It is hopeless. I am further away now than ever. It has gone. I can conjure . . . nothing.

Drowning. The fear is of drowning (now the tears come, now they come). I see water and the lilies and the reeds and the weeds and unless I can understand all that then I am as dead. I have come too close. I have deadened myself with that last word. I killed my pain and my memory. I typed myself dead. I have begun to rock back and forth again and I have also understood a kind of blocking to the flow of my writing. Very strange that, even when I am writing on remote things there is a microdread at my fingers ends, a kind of reflex resistance which forestalls me as I go (it senses. 'I' don't sense but 'it' does) and it sends me off in another direction. I just had a sudden intimation of just how free I am doing this it really is infinite and I know that if I go on long enough then I shall have to meet it somewhere along the way and when 'it' (what?) senses this it makes me stop. Writing then is full of dangers. No wonder that I resist it so. No wonder that I fear it, put it off. By the slightest error in the mechanisms of distance I may at any moment be pitched into memory and into hysteria. I write, therefore along the inner edge of hysteria *all the time* without, up to now, ever knowing it. I remain this side of it by being a literary critic. For in that kind of writing the distance is perfectly manageable. There is no fear involved, merely the subconscious effort of steering away from the matter of my own mind, the modality of consciousness which threatens me more than any other: memory.

And yet of course I know that unless I come to terms with those memories all is a mask, a screen. There is only the insubstantial smokescreen to my cowardice or my phobic drive. I write to escape the memories even though by a slight deviation in rhythm or cadence I shall be suddenly standing right next to them. Yet auto-analysis is such a poor thing. Interesting only to my own thirsty ego. And whilst I am always looking over my own shoulder for praise and acclaim I shall not be able to write one honest word, not one word of truth. It is hope less. I am further away now than ever. It has gone. I can conjure . . . nothing.

3 L'Éclatement du sujet: The Work of Julia Kristeva

> How could he say 'I' when he was something new and
> unknown, not himself at all? This I, this old formula of
> the age, was a dead letter.
>
> (*Women in Love*)

As Plato tells us in the *Cratylus*, the *Sophist*, and in *Letter
VII*,[1] there is no *logos* which does not presuppose the interlacing of names with verbs: syntax is the condition of coherence of rationality. Any disturbance of syntactic order or its
elements destabilizes the relations of reason and calls into
question the fixed boundaries of subject and object, cause
and condition. It is on this account that the loss of syntactic
coherence has been taken as an indication of insanity.[2] The
inability to fix pronouns in place and to keep their designa-
tion constant, the inability to follow the grammatical rules
for negating, making a phrase passive or conditional, or
ordering the unities of subject and object in a sentence, these
inabilities token the collapse of mental order and of symbolic
control. For our purposes, they also token something more
general which pertains even in cases when agrammaticality is
not so drastic: any modifications in language, particularly
infractions of syntactic laws, are a modification of the status
of the subject (p. 13).

First published in 'Exposition and Critique of Julia Kristeva', stencilled occasional paper
(General Series: SP No. 49), Centre for Contemporary Cultural Studies, University of Birm-
ingham, 1977. All references in brackets are to Kristeva's *La Révolution du langage poétique*
(Paris, 1974).
    [1] *Cratylus*, 425a, in *The Dialogues of Plato*, trans. B. Jowett, ed. R. M. Hare and D. H.
Russell (London, 1970), iii. 176; *The Sophist*, trans. and introd. A. E. Taylor, ed. R. Kliban-
sky and E. Anscombe (London, 1961), 173–4; *Letter VII*, in *Plato: Collected Dialogues*, ed.
E. Hamilton and H. Cairns (Princeton, NJ, 1963), 1589–91.
    [2] Aphasia is the traditional testing ground for the study of the interrelation of syntactic
selection and mental malfunction. The most celebrated case was that of 'Schneider' analysed
by Gelb and Goldstein, *Psychologische Analysen hirnopathologischer Fälle* (Leipzig, 1920).

To invoke Plato at the outset is not conventional piety: the philosophic rationalism which begins with Plato and which continues with uneven but massive force through to the present day has been a dominant and incisive model of what constitutes 'being human', *anthropos* as *logos*. It is the tradition which, present in Aquinas and central in Bacon, Descartes, Locke, and Kant, leads through to the philosophic concern of our century with the relation between language and logic. An acceptance of the notion that human understanding and the understanding of the human must focus its analysis on the interlacing of names with verbs—on language as the bearer of logical relations and hence the articulation of the structure of mind. An acceptance of this notion is the grounding supposition of modern philosophy, particularly logical positivism and its offshoots, but also the phenomenology of Brentano.

The position ascribed to the subject in this tradition, though often left unspoken, is clearly that of a singular, transcendental *unity*. Its clearest expression is perhaps in Kant's *Critique of Pure Reason* when Kant considers the unity of apperception:

To know anything in space (for instance, a line), I must *draw* it, and thus synthetically bring into being a determinate combination of the given manifold, so that the unity of this act is at the same time the unity of consciousness (as in the concept of a line); and it is through this unity of consciousness that an object (a determinate space) is first known. The synthetic unity of consciousness is, therefore, an objective condition of all knowledge. It is not merely a condition that I myself require in knowing an object, but is a condition under which every intuition must stand in order *to become an object for me*. For otherwise, in the absence of this synthesis, the manifold would *not* be united in one consciousness.[3]

The identification of consciousness with a synthetic unity of mental action means that the ego constitutes itself as a whole, as a self, which stabilizes the otherwise dispersed and contradictory perspectives of a being which has no fixed or

---

[3] Kant, *Critique of Pure Reason*, trans. Norman Kemp Smith (London, 1929; repr. 1973), B 138.

unified position. Modern linguistic philosophy (Frege, Carnap, Russell, Wittgenstein, through to Quine and Strawson) explores this concatenation of syntax, logic, and reference which unifies, and yet is made possible by, a homogeneous, singular subject. Wittgenstein's double assertion in the *Tractatus*—'The limits of my language mean the limits of my world . . . Logic pervades the world: the limits of the world are also its limits'[4]—makes language, logic, and the world coterminous. The limits of my world, of what *is for me*, are made identical to the limits imposed by linguistic and rational order.

This rationalist project, with its attendant notion of the subject as a synthesizing unity, as the unique guarantee of *being*, is as dominant in modern linguistics as it is in philosophy. Nicely marked in Chomsky's *Cartesian Linguistics*[5] by the title of the book itself, Chomsky argues that the supporting subject of syntactic order is in the Cartesian tradition of a unified *cogito*. Again, in post-Saussurean linguistics, Benveniste, writing on the pronominal opposition of Je/Vous, puts it thus: 'This polarity does not mean either equality or symmetry: the "I" always has a position of transcendence with respect to the "thou".'[6]

Thus both the Chomskian and the Saussurean conceptions of the subject in language accept the rationalist description of a transcendental ego, and thus both belong, in this respect at least, to that philosophic tradition which goes back via Kant and Descartes to Plato. Kristeva calls this conception of the subject thetic, since it is characterized by the laying-down or setting-forth (Gk, 'such as is placed') of positive statements or propositions. The thetic conception considers subjectivity as a unified consciousness able to produce reason through the propositional structures embedded in syntactic order.

[4] L. Wittgenstein, *Tractatus Logico-Philosophicus*, trans. D. F. Pears and B. F. McGuinness (London, 1961), 114–15, proposition 5.6 ('Die Grenzen meiner Sprache bedeuten die Grenzen meiner Welt') and 5.61 ('Die Logik erfüllt die Welt; die Grenzen der Welt sind auch ihre Grenzen').

[5] N. Chomsky, *Cartesian Linguistics* (New York, 1966).

[6] 'Cette polarité ne signifie ni égalité ni symétrie: l'"ego" a toujours une position de transcendance à l'égard de tu.' E. Benveniste, 'La Subjectivité dans le langage', in *Problèmes de linguistique générale* (Paris, 1966), 260.

But for at least as long as it has existed, this thetic tradition of high rationalism has been mocked and haunted by alien spirits. From the outset, Plato had to exclude most of music and literature from the realms of *The Republic*,[7] deleting from literature all horrifying and frightening names in the underworld, all gloomy accounts of the afterlife, all laments and unjust misery, all laughter, lies, and intemperate desire for the pleasures of eating, drinking, and sex. Madness and the representation of madness were also forbidden, and in music all the modes except two, which represent 'courage and moderation in good fortune or in bad', were likewise forbidden in the kingdom of philosophy. In other words, Plato feels his rational and unified Republic threatened from within by forces, desires, and activities which must be censored or ostracized if the rational state is to be maintained. A closer look at the nature of these threatening forces reveals that what Plato has to exclude as dangerous are the desire for sensual pleasure, laughter, the representatives of death and of madness, and those two art forms, music and literature, which may express or incite these subversive powers. What are excluded, then, are precisely those aspects of human activity which were to become the great themes of Freudian psychoanalysis; though it must be added that Freud's well-known dislike of music led to its being under-represented in his theoretical writings.

The correspondence is not accidental. The schism which Plato introduced between a harmonious rationality, on the one hand, and disruptive forces of passion, wit, death, and pleasure, on the other hand, has marked every major Western conception of the human. Nietzsche, by borrowing the terms Apollonian and Dionysiac, puts the origin of the representation of the schism even further back than Plato, but it is Plato who first begins to theorize the disjunction between them by favouring a dominant rationalism at the expense of these other, potentially disruptive powers. The problem for

---

[7] Plato, *The Republic*, trans. and introd. H. D. P. Lee (London, 1955), 114–38 (literature), 138–41 (music).

any thinker who does not merely champion one of these sides in a simple-minded way is to attempt *to think the relations between them*, to comprehend (in both its senses) the rational and the irrational, the sentence and the song.

It is this massive project which Julia Kristeva attempts in *La Révolution du langage poétique*. Her work is situated in the dialectic between formalist, passive, 'objective' theories of language and mind, on the one hand, and active, psychoanalytical theories of subjectivity, on the other, which together are attacked, synthesized, and transposed to produce a new concept of subjectivity and its place in language and poetic literature. Poetry is the focus of the work because the space occupied by poetry is poised directly over the schism which Plato opened up, the deep fissure between the thetic and those practices and impulses which threaten the thetic. Literature is the *lieu privilégié* of analysis because it has revealed at certain times, in the practice of its writing, the destruction which is wrought upon the thetic by a number of extra-rational phenomena—the disposition of basic impulses, desires, and fears which can be seen only in the degree to which they alter the logical, propositional nature of normal communication.

This tension between the thetic and what for the moment I will term simply the non-thetic, is not an eternal war waged in a vacuum. It has determinate historical and social forms which arise from the particular ways in which the *activity* of writers, caught up in the network of social meaning systems, *transforms* and *challenges* the tradition which fails to contain that subjective activity. Literature, Kristeva argues,[8] not only shows us how language works in disposing of the particular pattern of thetic against non-thetic in a text, it is also an activity which brings the laws of established discourse into question, and thereby presents itself as a terrain where new sorts of discourse may be engendered. And since, as I argued in my first paragraph, a change in discourse is a change in the status of the subject, a radical new poetic discourse may

---

[8] Julia Kristeva, *Recherches pour une sémanalyse* (Paris, 1969).

produce a radical new status for the subject. But we must first recover much more of Kristeva's argument before such a statement becomes clear.

Kristeva's first object of attack is the thetic tradition of a single, unified subject, embodied in philosophy, linguistics, and also in those types of literature centred on mimetic and narrative representation (which not unnaturally turns out to be most of literature). Of course Kristeva's is only the last in a long line of such attacks, and substantially she is in agreement with both the sociological critique of the thetic (particularly as argued by Marx and Durkheim) and with the psychological critique (as argued by Freud, Lacan, and, in some qualified respects, by Marcuse and Reich). In a way it would not be inaccurate to see Kristeva's project as a reworking of both the Freudian and the Marxist notions of an active subject, as revealed in the modernist poetic activity, and mediated by a considerably revised version of modern linguistics.

The sociological critique of the thetic has become an intellectual reflex of our century. Meaning is not produced *within* a subject, but *between* subjects, in group, class, and society. And meaning is not simply given, everywhere and always, in the singular bond between one mind and the world of objects: it is produced, it has a history in the forms of modes of its production, both in the socialization of the child and in the transformations of culture. The cognition goes back at least to Hamann's *Vermischte Anmerkungen* (Miscellaneous Observations) of 1761,[9] in which the kinship of linguistic and economic systems of exchange is proposed as a way of explaining both. Production, whether of objects or meanings, is social, a *mode* of production, and Kristeva agrees that it was necessary for Marx to emphasize this in iconoclastic opposition to the bourgeois concept of work as purely individual and personal.[10] She quotes Derrida with approval when he writes that

---

[9] See particularly G. Steiner, *After Babel: Aspects of Language and Translation* (Oxford, 1975), 77.

[10] Kristeva, *Recherches pour une sémanalyse*, 35–7.

Money replaces things by their signs. Not only within a society but between one culture and another, or between one economic organization and another. That is why the alphabet is mercantile. It has to be understood in the monetary moment of economic rationality. The critical description of money is the faithful reflection of discourse on writing.[11]

For Marx, work could only be grasped in the values—of use or exchange—into which it was crystallized. Work represents nothing outside of the values in which it is stored up, for it is only in these values that it can be *measured* and hence enter into society and into theory. Work takes on a determinate form, and thus takes on *meaning*, only when it has already entered the system of exchange as a particular amount of production. Labour itself, anterior to exchange, remains in Marx the foundation of his theory, but unthinkable except as an infinite potential of available physical and mental expenditure. But, Kristeva says, labour itself *has* become thinkable as a concept, even when it is anterior to exchange. For Kristeva, this pure activity of the human body is 'mute'—for it is logically antecedent to exchange and cannot therefore embody value—but must exist as the subject's praxis and expenditure which is taken up by communication, by exchange, by determinate production, by meaning. Work cannot simply be a mode of production, but it must also be, simultaneously, subjective expenditure of effort, working itself through the mode of production. The two aspects have to be thought at once if the subject is not to be left as a blank, a passive, empty bearer of the social processes.

According to Kristeva, it is Freud's concept of work in the *Traumarbeit* which fills this blank and gives us the method to think through this 'production anterior to production', the disposition of subjective expenditure. Freud uncovers production itself as a process,[12] and as a particular semiotic system,

---

[11] 'L'argent remplace les choses par leurs signes. Non seulement à l'intérieur d'une société mais d'une culture à l'autre, ou d'une organisation économique à l'autre. C'est pourquoi l'alphabet est commerçant. Il doit être compris dans le moment monétaire de la rationalité économique. La description critique de l'argent est la réflexion fidèle du discours sur l'écriture.' J. Derrida, *De la grammatologie* (Paris, 1967), 424.

[12] Kristeva, *Recherches pour une sémanalyse*, 38.

a permutation of elements which models production and which is distinct from that of exchange. Kristeva thus wants to take account of Marxist, logical-philosophical, and Freudian theories of the subject—the sociological, rationalist, and psychological—but without collapsing the subject into any one of them. Her description of the subject thus draws on all three, but the central place is undoubtedly that of Freudianism recast in the light of Lacan. She conceives this human subjectivity as follows.

First of all (both in terms of the child and logically) to be human is to be a psychobiological entity energized by the movements and rhythms of impulses. The impulses are not only bio-energic charges but also psychic marks (p. 23) and their disposition across the mind and body is called a *chora* (χώρα, space, room, place, locality).

The *chora* is a non-expressive totality, constituted by the impulses and their stasis in a 'figured movement' which is gradually regulated by the constraints imposed upon the body by family and society. At this rudimentary stage it is hardly anything more than a certain rhythm, and its only analogy is body or vocalic movement. Kristeva follows Melanie Klein[13] in considering the oral and anal impulses the dominant ones, both structured and directed in relation to the body of the other (pp. 26–7), in a pre-Oedipal phase in which boys and girls *alike* view the mother as the receptacle of all that is desirable. The *chora* is the pre-socialized *space of motility* which makes gesture, phonic articulation, and chromatic identification possible. Gradually, under the constraints of biological growth and family structure, this *chora* becomes limited and provisionally fixed (p. 28) into the different semiotic materials—sound, movement, colour, and shape—so that it takes on a sort of economy of functions in relation to its contexts. This discharge of energy, which binds and orients the child to the mother, is always double, always both productive and destructive (p. 26), and in its doubleness may be likened to the double helix of the DNA

---

[13] M. Klein, in the French translation used by Kristeva, *La Psychanalyse des enfants* (Paris, 1969).

molecule. The *chora* is thus the space of operation of sensory-motor impulses, both positive and negative in the degree to which they settle into a pattern but also destroy the stability of that pattern's new movements (p. 27). Because of this constant movement, there is no subject or personality at this stage, merely an unstable and provisional 'beating out' (*frayage*) of certain pathways and connections, the establishments of differences, parts of the body, the operation of vocal and anal sphincters, the focusing of the eyes, and so forth.

All these processes constitute the basis for language and form a crucial category in Kristeva's work, what she calls (perversely in view of its many other meanings) the semiotic. The semiotic is the production of sounds, rhythms, vocal and gestural modulations (such as intonation), *but anterior to meaning*, that is to say, before lexical and syntactic organization:

> This type of relations seems to us to be capable of specifying the *semiotic* as the psychosomatic modality of the process of 'signifiance', i.e. not symbolic but articulating (in the widest sense of the word articulation) a continuum . . . All these processes and relations, pre-sign and pre-syntax, have now been placed in a genetic perspective, as preliminary and necessary to language acquisition, from which they remain distinct. (p. 28)[14]

The semiotic then is the pre-condition for communication and language proper. It is both the ability of the baby to produce movement and differences in voice and gesture, and, more importantly, the rhythmic and phonic modulations which, though chronologically earlier than speech, always accompany speech as its material and psychophysical grounding throughout adult life. Even in the highest flights of rational thought, this semiotic basis is the necessary accompaniment and continuum. But in dreams, and in cer-

---

[14] 'Ce type de relations nous paraît susceptible de préciser le *sémiotique* en tant que modalité psychosomatique du procès de la signifiance, c'est-à-dire non symbolique mais articulant (au sens le plus large du terme d'articulation) un continuum . . . Tous ces processus et relations, pré-signe et pré-syntaxe, viennent d'être placés dans une optique génétique, comme préalables et nécessaires à l'acquisition du langage avec lequel ils ne se confondent pas.'

tain modern literary texts, it actually becomes dominant and breaks through the thetic part of language: 'However, it is only through the logic of the *dream* that they [these processes and relations] have been able to attract attention, and it is only in certain signifying practices, such as that of the *text*, that they dominate the process of signifiance' (p. 28).[15] Any innate, genetic traits find their place here, in the semiotic, the ordering and disposing of primary processes such as displacement and condensation, absorption and repression, rejection and stasis, all the processes which are the innate pre-conditions in the species for the acquisition of language (p. 29). In a sense, this semiotic order is pure musicality. It is rhythm, tonal difference, phonic change, movement of the body and of the limbs. This semiotic area, characterized as enigmatic, indifferent to language, feminine, a semiotic rhythm, is a sort of orchestration of primary movements and functions, what Mallarmé called a 'Mystère dans les lettres' (p. 29). Since it is anterior to signs and syntax—anterior to conscious communication—it is, quite literally, the unconscious, and it is at this point that the link with Freud becomes visible:

It can be seen that our positing of the semiotic is inseparable from a theory of the subject which takes account of Freud's positing of the unconscious. Decentring the transcendental *ego*, cutting it and opening it up to a dialectic in which its syntactic and categorical *understanding* is only the *threshold* moment, itself always *enacted* by the relation to the author that is dominated by the death instinct and its reiteration which produces 'signifier': that is how this subject appears to us in language. (p. 30, my emphasis)[16]

The reference to the death instinct (*la pulsion de mort*) is central in Kristeva's thinking on the nature of the *chora* and

---

[15] 'Ce n'est pourtant que par le logique du *rêve* qu'ils ont pu attirer l'attention, et ce n'est que dans certaines pratiques signifiantes, comme celle du *texte*, qu'ils dominent le procès de la signifiance.'

[16] 'Notre position du sémiotique est, on le voit, inséparable d'une théorie du sujet qui tient compte de la position freudienne de l'inconscient. Décentrant l'*ego* transcendental, le coupant et l'ouvrant à une dialectique dans laquelle son entendement syntaxique et categoriel n'est que le moment liminaire du procès, lui-même toujours agi par le rapport à l'autre que domine la pulsion de mort et sa réitération productrice de "signifiant": tel nous apparaît ce sujet dans le langage.'

its semiotic expression (even though it must be counted as the most controversial and least supported of Freudian concepts[17]). The *chora* is described as the place of articulation of the death instinct *across* primary narcissism and the desire for pleasure of the subject, this transversality disrupting his identity so that new psychic patterns are beaten out. The death instinct is the tendency of the organism to return to a homoeostatic state, rest and equilibrium, whilst the desire for pleasure drives against this stasis. But Kristeva gives a priority to the importance of the death instinct by saying that pleasure and narcissism are simply provisional positions against which the death instinct pushes, the resulting pressures creating new mental passages. Narcissism and pleasure are thus the 'inveigling and realization of the death instinct' (p. 27 n.).

Kristeva also links the Freudian idea of a death instinct with a more philosophical conception which she shares with Jacques Derrida.[18] Death is nothing other than a destruction of identity (in both the Hegelian and everyday meaning of the word) and is thus *negation* and *difference* with relation to a given subject. Kristeva thus writes about *la pulsion de mort* as negativity or rejection, any force which tends to *destroy the constituted identity of the subject*, even though this may have only a metaphorical relation to 'death' in the commonly conceived notion of the word.

The *chora* then is the 'space of motility' which engenders the semiotic, the grounding of signification in vocalic and corporal movement before it can make signs and sentences. Its nearest representations are the babble of the child and the rhythms of music.

[17] The death instinct was developed relatively late in the works of Freud and was first introduced in *Beyond the Pleasure Principle* in 1920. It has not managed to gain the acceptance of his disciples and successors in the way that his other theoretical concepts have. It unites the fundamental tendency of every living thing to return to its inorganic state with the destructive tendency (as revealed for example in sado-masochism) of the subject. It is this latter link of which Kristeva makes use in considering Lautréamont and Mallarmé.

[18] Derrida's course of seminars at the École Normale Supérieure for 1975–6 were on the philosophy of life and death, 'La Vie la mort'. In these seminars Derrida attacked, from a philosophical point of view, the biological writings on the subject, particularly the influential works of the Nobel prizewinner, François Jacob. But the linkage of thought on the subject of death between Derrida and Kristeva can best be seen in *L'Écriture et la différence* (Paris, 1967), 301.

This semiotic layer does not disappear when the child learns to speak, but on the contrary remains as the necessary basis of articulation and sense. It is what drives language on and makes it possible. Language can never be simply a passive set of protocols and structures—though this is usually the way it is envisaged by modern linguistics—but it must be a praxis, an activity and process which is motivated by the psychobiological disposition of the speaking subject.

The next question to which Kristeva addresses herself is how, on the basis of this semiotic *chora*, the thetic (logical, judging, naming) part of subjectivity may be produced. Kristeva subsumes all the logical, predicative, syntaxic aspects of language under one term which, again demonstrating a wilful perversity in the face of accepted usage, she terms the symbolic. The symbolic is an extension of the thetic discussed above, it is that major part of language which names and relates things, it is that unity of semantic and syntactic competence which allows communication and rationality to appear. Kristeva has thus divided language into two vast realms, the semiotic—sound, rhythm, and movement, anterior to sense and linked closely to the impulses (Triebe)—and the symbolic—the semantico-syntactic function of language necessary to all rational communication about the world. The latter, the symbolic, usually 'takes charge of' the semiotic and binds it into syntax and phonemes, but it can only do so on the basis of the sounds and movements presented to it by the semiotic. The dialectic of the two parts of language form the *mise-en-scène* of Kristeva's description of poetics, subjectivity, and revolution.

To even ask the question 'How is the symbolic produced?', one has already delivered a direct challenge to much rationalist-based philosophy. Instead of accepting the thetic notion of subjectivity as a given, defining what may be judged as subjectivity by remaining exclusively in the realm of predication, and analysing its structure, Kristeva displaces it from its accepted centrality, to show that it is a produced stage in the development of subjectivity, bound to, and articulated upon, another stage which makes it possible, and which is neither the realm of objects nor the directly social, but *also* a part of subjectivity. The transcendental ego of Kant and modern logic suddenly finds that it is not alone, nor sovereign, as it had always thought. But this is emphatically not to say that the notion of a transcendental ego may now be jettisoned in favour of an heterogeneous concept of mind. What was wrong was not the argument that a unified subject was necessary to the unity of apperception and hence to the logic of predication: such an argument must necessarily hold true. But it is wrong to make *this* transcendental ego coextensive with subjectivity as such, rather than a *produced stage* within it. Kristeva does not seek to destroy the philosophic concept of the thetic, nor the weight of logical and linguistic philosophy based upon it, but she seeks to decentre the concept by accommodating it within a subjectivity which has an unconscious, psychobiological drives, and a history:

Modern philosophy concurs in recognizing that it is the transcendental ego that has the right to represent the *thesis* which sets up signification (sign and/or proposition). But it is only since Freud that the question can be posed not only as to the origin of this thesis, but as to the process of its production. If one simply stigmatizes the thetic as the basis of metaphysics, one is liable to be merely its antichamber unless one specifies the conditions for the production of this thesis. Freud's theory of the unconscious and its development by Lacan seem to us to be a revelation of the fact that thetic signification is a phase that is producible in certain definite conditions during the process of 'signifiance', that it constitutes the subject without being reducible to its process, because it is the threshold of language. (p. 43)[19]

Kristeva distinguishes, therefore, between the semiotic (the impulses and their articulation) (p. 41) and the domain of

[19] 'La philosophie moderne est d'accord pour reconnaître que c'est à l'ego transcendental que revient le droit de représenter la *thèse* instauratrice de la signification (signe et/ou proposition). Mais c'est seulement à partir de Freud que la question peut être posée non sur l'origine de cette thèse, mais sur le procès de sa production. A stigmatiser dans le thétique le fondement de la métaphysique, on s'expose à être son anti-chambre; à moins de spécifier les conditions de production de cette thèse. La théorie freudienne de l'inconscient et son développement lacanien nous paraissent être précisément une mise à jour du fait que la signification thétique est une stade productible dans certaines conditions précises lors du procès de la signifiance, qu'elle constitue le sujet sans se reduire à son procès, puisqu'elle est le seuil du langage.'

signification, the symbolic, which is always a domain of propositions or judgements, that is to say, a domain of *positions*. This positionality, the ability to take up a point of view (explored by Husserl in his phenomenological reduction) is what installs the *identity* of the subject and of his objects, identity being a separation which the subject achieves between the image of himself and the image of the world. He becomes conscious of himself as a *self,* and of the world as a world of objects and of other subjects separate from himself. This coming-to-consciousness is actually an identifiable period in the growth of the child, and is signalled by his ability to produce holophrastic utterances, which are probably not always fully formed sentences (NP–VP) as conceived by generative grammar, but differ from the babble of an earlier phase in that they separate out a subject from an object and attribute to it some fragment of meaning (as, for example, when the cat goes 'miaow' and all animal are then designated 'miaows').

The mechanisms which produce this symbolic and hence thetic level of identity and signification are the mirror phase[20] and the castration complex.

It is the mirror phase, which produces the child's 'spatial intuition', that is at the heart of signification (and which accounts for the fact that the spatial metaphor is the dominant organizing metaphor in language). The mirror phase, taken from Lacan, designates, in a way that is partly literal and partly metaphorical, the point in a child's development when, fascinated by its own image in a mirror, it recognizes the reversed image of a self. This visual image of himself is the first time that the child conceives of himself in his imagination as a totality separated from the rest of the world. It is the necessary pre-condition for the child to be able to say 'me' or 'I', as well as being the visual image which stands as the prototype for the world of objects.[21] The mirror phase

[20] For the mirror phase, see 'Le Stade du miroir', in J. Lacan, *Écrits* (Paris, 1966), 95 ff. This difficult essay by a notoriously complex writer can be usefully supplemented by the discussion of the mirror stage in A. Wilden, *The Language of the Self* (Baltimore, 1968), to which I am indebted in this section of my exposition. See also *New Left Review*, 51 (Sept.–Oct. 1968).

[21] Lacan, 'Subversion du sujet et dialectique du désir', in *Écrits*, 822.

inaugurates the position–separation–identification which permits the formation of sentences and propositions.

The mirror phase may be decomposed into three separate
moments. At first, the child perceives the image in the mirror
as a real being whom he tries to grasp or approach. He
reacts to this image by jubilatory mimicry, and what is indi-
cated at this stage is the recognition of the body-image of
another *as a whole*. Lacan writes:

> The total form of the body through which the subject overtakes in
> a mirage the maturing of his potency is only given to him as a
> *Gestalt*, i.e. in an eternality in which, to be sure, that form is more
> constituting than constituted but where, above all, it appears to
> him in a relief of stature which fixes it and in a symmetry which
> inverts it, as opposed to the turbulence of movement with which he
> feels himself animate it.[22]

At first the *Gestalt* offers an image of the body which is
quite opposed to the 'turbulent movement' which the child
himself feels. But before very long the child discovers that the
image is nothing but an image. He no longer seeks to seize
it, nor does he search for the other behind the mirror,
because he realizes that there is *no-body*. Thirdly, the child
recognizes not simply an image but *his* image in the specular
reflection of himself. In this moment of recognition he has, to
a degree which is close to being literal, realized an image of
himself, he has grasped his own appearance, the image that
he makes for/of himself, as a produced identity, a conquest
of his body as a unity and as an image. It is this identification and unification of a self as a self's image which is
important for the generation of a unified consciousness capable of producing speech. Anthony Wilden writes: 'The central concept of the mirror phase is clear: this primordial
experience is symptomatic of what makes the *moi* an imaginary construct. The ego is an *Idealich*, another self, and the

---

[22] 'C'est que la forme totale du corps par quoi le sujet devance dans un mirage la matu-
ration de sa puissance, ne lui est donnée que comme *Gestalt*, c'est-à-dire dans une extérior-
ité, où certes cette forme est-elle plus constituante que constituée, mais où surtout elle lui
apparaît dans un relief de stature qui la fige et sous une symétrie qui l'inverse, en opposition
à la turbulence de mouvement dont il s'éprouve l'animer.' Lacan, *Écrits*, 95.

stade du miroir is the source of all later identifications.'[23] The total image of the body, set over against a realm of otherness, is thus the moment of production and structuration of an identity through the mediation of the body-image. The transcendental ego necessary to logical and rational communication and action comes into play during the mirror phase. Confirmation of this comes from another source, and lends considerable support to Lacan's theory.

The image of the body in bits and pieces, *le corps morcelé*, is one of the most common of dreams, fantasies, certain types of schizophrenia, experience of drugs and art and literature. The works of Hieronymus Bosch, Salvador Dali, and Artaud express the notion clearly. This corporal disintegration is the reverse of the constitution of the body during the mirror phase, and it occurs only at those times when the unified and transcendent ego is threatened with dissolution. The way in which the fantasy of the fragmented body accompanies the breakdown of rational sovereignty is the clear complement of Lacan's idea that the image of the total body is necessary to the creation of rational unity. In each case, the image of the body, of the self, mediates thetic unity and disintegration.

For Kristeva, the fear of castration finishes off (*parachève*) this process (p. 44). The argument becomes a little murky at this point (pp. 45–50) but, as I read it, the castration complex has two effects which further the installation of the symbolic. First, the mother, hitherto the receptacle and receiver of every demand from the child, is separated from the child (by (1) the gradual cessation of weaning and (2) the gradual intervention of the father), which has the effect of detaching the child from its dependence and identity with the mother, thus opening up a *lack*, an absence of that-which-is-desired which can only be represented by a figurative substitute, an image or representation. Speech arises as an attempt to fill this lack, this *béance* towards the absent object (in this case the mother). At the epistemological level, the 'lack of an

---

[23] Wilden, *The Language of the Self*, 160.

object' is the gap in the signifying chain which the subject seeks to fill at the level of the signifier.

Secondly, the separation from the mother now makes her into an 'other', someone for whom, and to whom, the speech is made and addressed. The speech is made for her and not for me, and it is thus that the other is established as posses-sor of, or space of, the signifier:

> The gap between the imaged ego and instinctual motility, between the mother and the demand addressed to her, is the very break which installs what Lacan calls the place of the Other as the place of the 'signifier'. The subject is masked by 'an ever purer signifier', but the lack of presence confers on *another* the role of holding the possibility of signification. (pp. 45–6)[24]

This moment of separation from the mother is a part of the castration complex because Kristeva, following Lacan, makes the mother an identification with the phallus ('c'est dire qu'elle est le phallus', p. 45). The child is 'cut off' from the immediate nurturing contact with the mother hitherto enjoyed with such close physical and mental bonding that there was neither need nor space for the establishment of communication about things. At the same time this period is when the sexuality of the child ceases to be 'polymorphous perverse' (the child as demanding sexual contact and pleasure for all parts of the body and irrespective of incest laws) and becomes specifically genital. The laws of incest (the Laws) always linguistically structured, are imposed at the same time (p. 45). It is this reference to incest prohibi-tion which completes the Oedipal triangle and completes the castration complex. The installation of symbolic lan-guage (thetic, naming, propositional) is what allows the imposition of the Law, the interdiction of the Mother as a focus of love, through the 'apprehension' (as both fear and learning) of the Paternal order. Lacan writes in his *Rome Discourse*:

---

[24] 'La béance entre l'ego imagé et la motilité pulsionnelle, entre la mère et la demande qui lui est adressée, est la coupure même qui instaure ce que Lacan appelle le lieu de l'Autre comme lieu du "signifiant". Le sujet est occulté "par une signifiant toujours plus pur", mais ce manque à y être confère à un *autre* le rôle de tenir la possibilité de la signification.'

The primordial Law is therefore that which in regulating marriage ties superimposes the kingdom of culture on that of nature abandoned to the law of copulation. The interdiction of incest is only its subjective pivot, revealed by the modern tendency to reduce to the mother and the sister the objects forbidden to the subject's choice, although full licence outside of there is not yet entirely open.

This law, therefore, is revealed clearly enough as identical to an order of language. For without kinship nominations, no power is capable of instituting the order of preferences and taboos which bind and weave the yarn of lineage down through succeeding generations . . . It is *in the name of the father* that we must recognize the support of the symbolic function which, from the dawn of history, has identified his person with the figure of the law.[25]

The mirror phase and the castration complex thus set up the second layer of language, the symbolic, which is language as communication proper, which names objects and expresses their relation to one another in the laws of syntax. The symbolic is thus generated by the birth of *desire* as it replaces the simple *demand* of the child and by the birth of *repression* (the Primary Repression of the Oedipal interdiction which prefigures all later repressions) as it replaces simple *rejection*. The two levels of signification, therefore, the semiotic and the symbolic, 'correspond' as forms of meaning to the maternal and paternal functions in the Oedipal relation which the child lives through as a condition of his growth. And just as an adult's sexual behaviour is rooted in his own particular experience of the Oedipal, his own produced configuration of identification and rejection of the figures of father and mother, so too the adult's particular subjectivity will be rooted in the specific intermixing of the semiotic and the symbolic, the rejection and acceptance of law incessantly weaving the particular dialectic of his personality. Active and passive, submission and aggression, rationality and passion spin out a pattern of loose and now tighter threads which, in their recurrence and repetitions, are the pattern of subjectivity. In other words, it is the *way in which* the semiotic relates to and disfigures the symbolic, as well as the *way in which*

---

[25] Lacan, in Wilden's translation, *The Language of the Self*.

the symbolic reasserts its unifying control of the semiotic, which gives us the basis of subjectivity as a process. From the mirror phase onwards the semiotic and the symbolic involve each other in a shifting process of dependence and rejection, the spreading reticulation of syntactic and nominal order are informed and sometimes broken by the power of the semiotic; the signifying power of desire, aggression, and pleasure are disposed according to the way the particular person has lived through the Oedipal complex and that experience is compulsively repeated in all his later psychic processes.

Kristeva thus reverses the normal way of thinking about the thetic consciousness. It is not some already constituted 'I' which produces coherent sentences about the world: on the contrary, it is the introduction of the child into the world of syntax which permits the development of that child as a unified subject, as a conscious 'I'. The thetic and the syntactic are inseparable and the production of subject and predicate, name and verb, or, to take up the terms of Strawson, 'feature concepts' and 'feature-placing statements', the production of the two major syntactic unities (the placed and the placing, the bound and the binding, the modified and the modifier are three ways in which these nominal and predicative functions have been described) enables the subject to achieve a stable position over against the world. The most significant result of this reversal is that *it is only in language that the 'I' exists, but this 'I' is not exhaustive of the subject who is producing the language.* There is always a difference between the subject as expressed *in* a sentence and the subject who *produces* the sentence, the former being a temporary position adopted within the process of the latter.

This distinction, drawing as it does on the familiar linguistic difference between the subject who speaks (*le sujet de l'énonciation*) and the subject of what is said (*le sujet de l'énoncé*) is an elegant solution to the dichotomy posed at the outset. These two different subjects correspond to the active, heterogeneous subject and the unified, thetic subject respectively, and together make up the process of self-production of subjectivity: 'Productive of the speaking subject, this making-other is accomplished on condition that it leaves outside itself, in the heterogeneous, that same speaking subject' (p. 55).[26] And again, further on in her exposition, Kristeva writes that 'The subject never *is*, the subject is only the *process of signifiance* and presents itself only as *signifying practice*, i.e. when it absents itself *in the position* from which social-historical-signifying activity unfolds' (p. 188).[27] If I write 'I sing the sofa', the 'I' of that sentence is not the same as the 'I' who produced the sentence even though it attempts to be so. It is logically impossible that the 'I' who sings the sofa may be coincident with and exhaustive of, the supposedly same 'I' that writes '"I" sing the sofa'. It must be some other self who is grasping the self as an object to write about, and Kristeva endorses and extends this familiar philosophical paradox by theorizing the mode of production of the first 'I' (the subject of what is said) by the second 'I' (the subject who speaks). The history of subjectivity is never the history of a subject always present to himself, but, on the contrary, a history of a process of capture and escape, stability and dissolution, a heterogeneous subject which is perpetually displacing its own established positions. The subject which supports syntax and makes it possible is necessarily absent from it, but when it does re-emerge it tends to perturb thetic calm by redistributing the signifying order, by altering syntax and by disrupting nominal groups. This is not to say that the sentence structure is destroyed, but it is pushed into an infinite variety of new forms, forms which Mallarmé, Lautréamont, and James Joyce were the first to produce and enjoy. These revolutionary textual forms effected a revolutionary conception of subjectivity which, according to Kristeva (p. 592), embodies a degree of freedom which will require 'at the best several centuries' to be fully realized in practical social terms:

[26] 'Productrice su sujet parlant, cette altération se réalise à condition de laisser hors d'elle, dans l'hétérogène, ce même sujet parlant.'

[27] 'Le sujet *n'est* jamais, le sujet n'est que *le procès de la signifiance* et ne se présente que comme *pratique signifiante*, c'est-à-dire lorsqu'il s'absente *dans la position* à partir de laquelle se déploie l'activité sociale-historique-signifiante.'

In art in general, and in the *text* more particularly from the end of the nineteenth century, there is constituted a language which speaks these sites of rupture which economistic class-consciousness represses, sites of rupture corresponding to the desire of the masses but unexpressed and perhaps inexpressible by them in productivist capitalist society in the state of industrialization, sites of rupture which are therefore withdrawn into the experience of the cultural elites and, within those elites, accessible to rare subjects in whom these breaks incur the risk and advantage of radicalizing themselves into madness or aestheticism and so of losing their ties with the social chain. That is what we wish to suggest.[28]

This claim evidently needs close scrutiny.

The relation of the semiotic to the symbolic is neither facile opposition nor simple dependence, and Kristeva never champions the one at the expense of the other. Though it is the energy, sound rhythm, and movement of the semiotic which grounds the word-foundation of the symbolic, the latter is nevertheless the condition of heterogeneity which continues to assure the stable position of the subject and, in deploying his semiotic 'musicality', assures the continuance of the subject as a source of meanings (pp. 62–83). The thetic is the threshold between the semiotic and the symbolic, and the essential point of Kristeva's theoretical position in *La Révolution du langage poétique* resides in this: that the modes of infusion between semiotic and symbolic across the thetic give us the forms of subjectivity, and whatever modes these may be, they become particularized and harden out into specific patterns of individuality through the psychic processes discovered by Freud and reformulated by Lacan. The relation to one's mother and father in the realm of the imaginary, fetishism, anal obsession, identification with the law (hysteria, p. 329) and rejection of all law (psychosis, p. 329), these

---

[28] 'Que dans l'art en général, et dans le *texte* plus particulièrement à partir de la fin du XIXe siècle, se constitue un langage qui parle ces lieux de rupture que la conscience de classe économiste refoule, lieux de rupture propres au désir des masses mais inexprimés et peut-être même inexprimables par elles dans la société capitaliste productiviste en état d'industrialisation, lieux de rupture donc retirés dans l'expérience des élites culturelles et, au sein de ses élites accessibles à de rares sujets chez qui ses ruptures courent le risque et l'avantage de se radicaliser jusqu'à la folie ou l'esthétisme et de perdre ainsi leurs attaches avec la chaîne sociale,—voilà ce que nous voudrions suggérer.' J. Kristeva, 'La Révolution du langage Poétique', *Tel Quel*, 56 (Winter 1973), 48.

are all modes through which the thetic may be transgressed to give a distinctive and recognizable type of subjectivity. The mode of transgression, or what Kristeva calls 'forclusion' following Lacan's translation of *Verwerfung* (rejection), is what distinguishes Mallarmé from Lautréamont and determines a particular type of subjectivity. The manifold processes whereby the semiotic may break through the symbolic, or whereby the symbolic assumes control of the semiotic, is transfixed by the forms of movement and displacement which take place across them both.

The role of poetic modernism in this process of subjective creation is paramount, since it is the *practice* of those inner unconscious movements of which *psychoanalysis* is the theory:

Then, in this socio-symbolic order thus saturated if not already closed, poetry—let us say more precisely, poetic language—recalls what always was its function: to introduce, across the symbolic, that which works on it, crosses it and threatens it. What the theory of the unconscious looks for, poetic language practices, within and against the social order: the ultimate means of its mutation or subversion, the condition for its survival and revolution. (p. 79)[29]

'Literature', in the writing of Lautréamont, Mallarmé, Artaud, Roussel, and Joyce, has been the refusal to conceal or repress the *signifier*, the material operation of language itself, even though it is the signifier which founds culture and signification. The 'burst unity' (*l'unité éclatée*) of *Chants de maldoror* and the *Poésies* of Lautréamont confront (or rather 'affront') the world of discourse in its constitutive laws, subverting its 'normal' and 'established' order, and, by disrupting it, opening out a revolutionary possibility for subjectivity within the new significatory processes. Not surprisingly, however, Kristeva remains uncertain about the exact nature of the relation between the disruption of normal fictional and

---

[29] 'Alors, dans cette ordre socio-symbolique ainsi saturé sinon déjà clos, la poésie—disons plus exactement le langage poétique—rappelle ce qui fut depuis toujours sa fonction: introduire, à travers le symbolique, ce qui le travaille, le traverse et le menace. Ce que la théorie de l'inconscient cherche, le langage poétique le pratique à l'intérieur et à l'encontre de l'ordre social: moyen ultime de sa mutation ou de sa subversion, condition de sa survie et de sa révolution.'

poetic practice on the one hand and the political, revolutionary disruption of social relations on the other. In its strong
form, Kristeva claims an *active*, determining correspondence
between the two, the pleasure and the violence, which breaks
the repressive laws of phallocentric logic at the level of the
subject, actively promoting revolutionary social change by
'overthrowing' the ensemblist logic which underpinned the
existing society:

there are texts which, in introducing the infinity of the process into
the constitutive elements of the linguistic system and into the finite
utterances of the social code (i.e. into the ideologemes which
express the socially coded relations of production and reproduction)
operate on the limits where the ensemblist logic of the social system
is put in danger . . . In this sense, and while remaining locked in
the house of the State, the poets, though 'minor sovereigns' or 'children of the house', nonetheless add to this a radical subversive role
which no other practice can assume. (p. 381)[30]

At other points, Kristeva's description of the role supposedly played by poetry in the transformation of bourgeois ideology is cast differently. She even puts an opposite argument
to the one just given and writes that, by an irony of assimila-
tion with which we are all familiar, the avant-garde of the
late nineteenth century served the needs of the dominant ideology by acting as a substitute for the repressed subjective
praxis that the society itself denied:

In thus abdicating the current social process, and while exhibiting a
moment that is repressed but constituent insofar as it exhibits the
moment dissolving all constituted unity, the 19th century avant-
garde text serves the dominant ideology since it supplies it with the
means of making up for its lacks, without directly challenging the
system of its reproduction in representation (in signification). (p.
186)[31]

[30] '. . . il y a des textes qui, en introduisant l'infinité du procès dans les éléments consti-
tutifs du système linguistique et dans les énoncés finis du code social (c'est-à-dire dans les
idéologèmes qui expriment les rapports de production et de reproduction socialement codés)
opèrent aux limites où la logique ensembliste du système social est mise en péril . . . En ce
sens, et tout en restant enfermés dans la maison étatique les "poètes", pour être des "sou-
verains mineurs" ou des "enfants de la maison", n'y ajoutent pas moins un rôle subversif
radical qu'aucune autre pratique ne peut assumer.'
[31] 'En abdiquant ainsi le processus social en cours, et tout en exhibant un moment

In another formulation, Lautréamont played a role of passive witness (*témoin*) to changes in the subject which 'correspond' (and it is the nature of this correspondence which is precisely in question here) to the social *éclatement* of the 1871 revolution:

Thus, *without denying the unity of reason* (of the symbolic and of the subject which it posits), but *ex-centring it*, affirming the subject as a contradiction, Lautréamont-Ducasse gives his texts a heroic, revolutionary connotation, which testifies, for the subject, to what the revolted masses of Paris will endeavour to do on the social scale in 1871. (p. 481)[32]

Of the many problems which Kristeva's work raises, the relation between formal literary 'revolution' of Mallarmé and Lautréamont and social revolutionary practice seems to me by far the most questionable. For Kristeva, the two writers are fundamentally important because they mounted attacks, from opposed but complementary directions, on phallocentric logic: Mallarmé, by identification with the mother (and through the form of his verse with the 'maternal', infinite genotext of the semiotic); Lautréamont by his violent, implacable attack on the father figure, law, and all forms of phallocentric domination. Mallarmé subverts, ruptures, and finally destroys the laws of syntax which are the guarantee of the laws of reason, the law of the father, and the laws of the state. Lautréamont, by permuting the shifters of the narrative in *Chants de maldoror*, breaks up the unity of subject found in traditional narrative forms with their sustained and clearly distinguished actants (the 'coherent' character of folk-tale and realist novel). Thus Lautréamont, too, disperses, from a complementary perspective, the unified, transcendent subject which had hitherto always underpinned phallocentric rationality.

refoulé mais constituant pour autant qu'il exhibe le moment dissolvant toute unité constituée, le texte avant-gardiste du XIXe siècle sert l'idéologie dominante puisqu'il lui fournit de quoi substituer à ses manques, sans mettre directement en cause le système de sa reproduction dans la représentation (dans la signification).'

[32] 'Ainsi, *sans dénier l'unité da la raison* (du symbolique et du sujet qu'il pose), mais en *l'excentrant*, en affirmant le sujet comme une contradiction, Lautréamont-Ducasse donne à ses textes une connotation héroïque, révolutionnaire, qui témoigne pour le sujet de ce que vont essayer à l'échelle sociale les masses révoltées de Paris.'

However, the step which Kristeva makes from this achieved poetic destruction of masculine rationality to political practice and feminism seems to me a deft sleight of pen, a merely sophistical linkage. The space between the formal textual innovations which she describes and the radical political practice (feminism) to which she subscribes is never satisfactorily filled, since the destruction of syntactic order and pronominal stability in a poetic discourse, even when it can be appropriated for political use, is always, and only, a negative politics, an evanescent disruption, incapable of identifying its own political agent (masculine or feminine).

In other words, the destruction of actantial position and pro-position in this poetic revolution can never have a positive vector, a political direction (direction is a function of stable identity). It always remains purified anarchism in a perpetual state of self-dispersal. And in this respect, it reveals its close material relation to the French left-academic context of its own production. Thus the form of *La Révolution du langage poétique*, a massive work within the philosophic tradition of the *doctorat d'état*, is evidently in contradiction with the content, a content manifestly hostile to the laws of the discourse in which the argument is cast. This argument is an appeal for an anarchist aesthetics, to displace the traditional sociology of literature across Lacanian psychoanalysis and recognizing in that process the formal novelties of the twentieth-century avant-garde as a crucial shift in our understanding of subjectivity. Upon this theoretical basis, the object of politics in general and feminism in particular is to follow the lead of this artistic avant-garde and achieve politically the destruction of the old, traditionally unified subject.

Kristeva has recently stated this link between theory and feminist praxis very clearly in an interview which she gave to *L'Espresso*, the Italian communist journal, in April 1977: 'I believe that the problem of the feminist movement today is that of inventing a form of anarchism which will express in behaviour and in action the discourse of the historical avant-garde: the destruction of the [traditional] Western subject.'[33] In this interview Céline and Pound are given as examples of what is here meant by the 'historical avant-garde', both, in their own way, having burst open the settled, unified subject underpinning 'masculine' bourgeois thought. Despite their ostensible fascism, Céline and Pound were, for Kristeva, substantially anti-fascist in their formal comprehension of its (psychological) origins ('I discorsi delle avanguardia artistiche sono stati i soli veri discorsi anti-fascisti con conoscenza (inconscia) di causa'). Feminism, according to Kristeva, thus has its political future mapped out along a route which leads back to *The Cantos*, a journey 'au bout de la nuit'. It is for feminists to discuss this project for themselves, and its anarchist grounding in the theoretical work outlined above. For myself, Kristeva's project is a brilliant essay in psycho-anarchic aesthetics, but which replaces a repressive, phallocentric *logos* by something far worse, a 'new' subject, drifting, dispersed, and as politically impotent as it is ever possible to be. An agent without agency, direction, or cohesion, neither *an sich* nor *für sich*, even more vulnerable to the force of social history than Ezra Pound, tearful, in his ward at St Elizabeth's asylum.

---

[33] 'Io credo che il problema del movimento femminile è oggi quello di diventare une forma dell'anarchismo che ritraduce in comportamenti e azione il discorso dell'avanguardia storica: la distruzione del soggetto occidentale.' J. Kristeva, *L'Espresso* (Apr. 1977), 63.

4 *Language and Location in Bleak House*

secretum iter et fallentis semita vitae

(Horace)

Behind the narrative of *Bleak House* stands another narrative, a
story of an earlier time, which as I read forward is gradually
revealed to me fragment by fragment. The narrative of *Bleak
House* is substantially the story of the partial, deferred revelation of this other story, concerning illicit love and an illegitimate baby girl. This brief, simple story is at the origin of *Bleak
House*, it is an anterior narrative of which the full narrative is
the complex reconstruction. The traces of this past episode
have been concealed and dispersed. The briefly united trinity
has been destroyed, the mother thinks the child dead, the
father is lost, and the child is an orphan. The relations
between the three of them are severed, and by the time of the
narrated opening of the novel all connection has been
obscured, leaving only tiny scraps of disconnected evidence in a
great fog.

The narrative structure of *Bleak House* describes both the
retracing of this earlier story and its important consequences as
they are brought into relation with one another. The recovery
of the secret gradually becomes an immense labour, involving
and implicating over seventy-five people, all of whom become
connected, in one way or another, with the distant initial
episode. The collecting of evidence, the search for traces and
fragments, and the piecing together of these in an endeavour to
know what happened, these acts of rediscovery and recovery
make the narrative largely retrospective, a movement forward
which is in fact a movement back and repeated *in knowledge*.

First published in *Critical Quarterly*, 20 (1978).

Indeed, repetition is the founding movement in *Bleak House*. The degree of repeating, mirroring, and recall is astonishing, and the whole novel is constructed on a doubling-up of figures, moments, and events which creates a reinforced connectedness. It is not simply that Inspector Bucket's investigation follows and doubles over that of Tulkinghorn, or that Krook is a parodistic Lord Chancellor, or that the picture of Lady Dedlock in Tony Jobling's room hangs over the mantelpiece in a strange, mocking double of the portrait at Chesney Wold. It is a kind of repetition which permeates most relations in the novel. The connections which gradually materialize between the initially isolated groups of characters are almost always of this same type: they are the retrospective recapture of a bond already established but temporarily obscured. The perfect Freudian type of this is the relation of mother to child, and the rediscovered bond between Esther and her mother is repeated in the rediscovered link between George and Mrs Rouncewell. When Esther sees Lady Dedlock's face it was 'like a broken glass to me, in which I saw scraps of old remembrance'. The realized and explicit linking of one character to another is like the recovery of some precious object lost under secrets or pressed back out of sight.

Esther's relations to Alan Woodcourt and Tom Jarndyce are exactly like this, the recovering, the rescue even, of an earlier established and endangered state. Her attraction for Woodcourt is given very early on in the novel (ch. 13) but is submerged by her dutiful relation to Jarndyce and only reemerges to become recognized and acknowledged by Esther right at the end of the novel. Her final acceptance of Woodcourt is the manifestation of a pre-established bond, an obscured remembrance, and is not something genuinely *new*. The love had always been there, it always already *was*, but its conscious recognition had been suppressed and delayed. Esther's connection to Jarndyce is of the same type, a return to origin, a return of the daughter to her 'father'. Initially Dickens makes it plain that they are substitute father and child: Jarndyce is called 'father', and the employment of a number of desexualized pseudonyms for Esther keeps her childlike. This relation is then threatened by Jarndyce's growing love for Esther with its distant hint of incest. When she now calls him 'father', it troubles him, and secrecy and reserve creep in to replace the open sincerity of the earlier, paternal relation. The termination of the novel is simply a reversion to the earlier state, the rediscovery of the lost paternal order, with Jarndyce playing proud father to his newly married daughter.

Again, the foundation of the second Bleak House is a recapitulation of this same movement, an act of closure which is a kind of refrain repeating the first theme. Jarndyce's construction of a second house, exactly upon the model of the first, with the same name and the same cosy, domestic security, is the perfect type of the relation which is in question. It is a repetition which, like Bucket's repetition of Tulkinghorn's investigation, not only repeats but revises the original in such a way as to improve it, to 'make it all better'. It is a process strikingly similar to the process of 'secondary revision' (*sekundare Bearbeitung*) described by Freud, and the romance termination of the novel is in this respect a compulsive repetition (*Wiederholungszwang*), the irresistible repeating of some previous pleasurable act. It is a termination by nostalgic re-cognition, an arrested movement in which progress and stability are fixed *in the past* without the possibility of supersession:

And still, as we went through the pretty rooms, out at the little rustic verandah doors and underneath the tiny wooden colonnades, garlanded and woodbine, jasmine and honeysuckle, I saw in the papering on the walls, in the colours of the furniture, in the arrangement of all the pretty objects, *my* little tastes and fancies, *my* little methods and inventions which they used to laugh at whilst they praised them, *my old ways everywhere*. (ch. 64)

It is in rediscovering and revealing 'old ways everywhere' that *Bleak House* gradually establishes a network of already latent connection which, in a narrative movement of constant return, hardens into the structure of stability and reference in the book.

Guppy's relation to Esther follows the pattern, an initial desire strongly rejected by Esther, a period of estrangement caused by her disfigurement, then the return of the desire and a second strong rejection echoing the first. Boythorn's initial relation to Sir Leicester as a sort of belligerent and affectionate antagonist in the tragi-comic legal wrangle over the right-of-way, is changed for a while at the death of Lady Dedlock, but resumes as before as the novel draws to its close. Lady Dedlock's second journey to the graveyard is a sort of compulsive, tragic re-enactment of the first, an obsessive return, like that to the doors of Chancery by Gridley, Richard, and Miss Flite, who says, 'There's a dreadful attraction in the place . . . There's a cruel attraction in the place. You *can't* leave it. And you *must* expect.' Mr and Mrs Badger hark back at every conversation to the two previous husbands in an amusing interlude based simply upon this same irresistible movement. And at the close of Esther's narrative we find Emma replacing Charley as Esther's maid in a detailed cameo of perfect, total repetition: 'So far as my small maid is concerned, I might suppose Time to have stood for seven years as still as the mill did half an hour ago; since little Emma, Charley's sister, is exactly what Charley used to be' (ch. 67).

It recalls the re-established relation between Jarndyce and Esther which follows a few paragraphs later: 'I have never lost my old names, nor has he lost his; nor do I ever, when he is with us, sit in any other place than in my old chair at his side. Dame Trot, Dame Durden, Little Woman!—all just the same as ever; and I answer, Yes, dear Guardian! just the same' (ch. 67).

Like the youthful beauty of Esther, which (somewhat surprisingly for the reader) comes back after her disfigurement, and like Mrs Bagnet's heroic lone journey *back* to her husband armed with only umbrella and cloak, there is a whole network of such 'returns', restored connections, which constitute the basis of security and truth in *Bleak House*, all 'just the same as ever'. Woodcourt's journey to the East, his illness, and subsequent return is another, paradigmatic instance. What this repetition achieves is an identification of aims and origins: the aim is to go back to the balanced, happy state which existed 'before all this business began', and it thereby posits a naïve theology of prelapsarian return. Heaven, for the dying Richard, is not an unknown future, but 'that pleasant country where the old times are' (ch. 65) so that, at this point, even Dickens's eschatology becomes a comforting analogue of the major repetitious structures in the narrative.

In systems analysis, this principle would be instantly recognized as homœostasis, the tendency of a system to return to the same state of equilibrium, a principle of conservative stability which restores it to what it was before. In Dickens this is a restored system of connections which wherever possible are re-established, if disrupted, as nearly as can be to their original identity. By the term 'connection' I mean two things simultaneously, the order of narrative and chronological connection (coherence, continuity) and also the nineteenth-century form of the word, 'connection', those private, intersubjective links between people bound by consanguinity, kinship, and close friendships. These two different meanings coalesce in *Bleak House* so that narrative and logical connection are inextricably joined to intersubjective connection, of which 'natural' family bonds are the highest type. It is the emergence of this pre-established system of twofold connection which is a founding order throughout the novel.

Early on, Dickens had explicitly posed the mystery of connection as a central term in *Bleak House*:

What connexion can there be, between the place in Lincolnshire, the house in town, the Mercury in powder, and the whereabouts of Jo the outlaw with the broom, who had that distant ray of light upon him when he swept the churchyard step? What connexion can there have been between many people in the innumerable histories of this world, who, from opposite sides of great gulfs, have, nevertheless, been very curiously brought together! (ch. 16)

It is the forging of this connection, particularly by repetition, by connecting back to an anterior moment of original fullness, which endures as a singular and indivisible formation in Dickens's writing. One can perceive in his work a kind of ethic of presence, what has been called in relation to Heidegger 'an ethic of nostalgia for origins, an ethic of archaic and natural innocence, or a purity of presence and self-presence in speech—an ethic, nostalgia, and even *remorse* . . .'.[1] The desire to go back and repeat is present everywhere in *Bleak House*, it is both an ethic—a preferred, valued form of action—and an ethos, a characteristic *disposition* of the text.

In certain respects, it is a kind of remorseful return. Turning back at a moment dominated by a mixture of guilt and regret, it is an attempt to return and correct a past which went wrong. Mr George's rediscovery of the mother he abandoned and neglected is a particularly remorseful form of a return to the maternal. Lady Dedlock's last journey, first to St Alban's to try and see her daughter, then back to the grave of her dead lover, is a poignant, distressing flight, activated by remorse of conscience. And of course there is Richard's return to Jarndyce, to his 'father' and guardian, a sad, confessional journey back which comes too late, though 'It will be like coming to the old Bleak House again' (ch. 65). In all three cases, the remorse is a mixture of guilt and self-blame which occurs when characters have broken their natural and dutiful 'connection' to others (connection in both its senses). The remorse is for a broken contract, for having destroyed or neglected the most valuable, enduring thing in Dickens's work, the close, mutual solidarity of kinship which finds its central expression in the bond between parent and child:

'George Rouncewell! O, my dear child, turn and look at me!' The trooper starts up, clasps his mother round the neck, and falls down on his knees before her. *Whether in a late repentance, whether in*

---

[1] J. Derrida on Martin Heidegger, quoted in the preface to the English translation of Derrida's *Of Grammatology*, trans. G. C. Spivak (Baltimore, 1976), p. xix.

the first association that comes back upon him, he puts his hands together as a child does when it says its prayers, and raising them towards her breast, bows down his head and cries. (ch. 55; my italics)

My reading of *Bleak House* is psychoanalytical only in a very general sense, but so much of the narrative is structured at the deepest level on this nostalgia for the innocent, the interdependence and connection of parent and child, of which the vast network in *Bleak House* is variously derivative. The remorse-filled trooper ('Grown such a man too, grown such a fine strong man') becomes once more a child raising his hands towards the maternal breast, and his tears, which mix shame and relief in the acceptance and forgiveness of his parent, are surely the same tears as those shed by Richard: 'My guardian Jarndyce saw what passed, came softly by me in a moment, and laid his hand on Richard's. "O Sir," said Richard, "you are a good man, you are a good man!" and burst into tears for the first time' (ch. 65).

The physical contact between parent and child, the boy's hand on his mother's breast and Richard's hand clasped by his 'father', is the duplicated, intimate gesture which seals and signifies the strongest possible unity of the two. No such strength of feeling is ever described between lovers in *Bleak House*. The relation between Esther and Woodcourt is pleasant and warmly appreciative, but appears distinctly tepid by comparison with the bond of child to 'parent'. The relation of Woodcourt to Jo when the latter is dying at the rifle range has a depth of pathos which engages Dickens's emotional powers far more than Woodcourt's relation to Esther. Ada's relation to Richard is straightforwardly maternal ('Ada leaned upon his pillow, holding his head upon her arm') as indeed is that of Caddy to her lover, Mr Turveydrop. Repetition in Dickens tends constantly to model itself on a recalling or remembrance of pre-Oedipal security and innocence, of which cries and a touching of the breast (quoted above) are the clearest index. The forms of repetition vary, the precise nature of the relation shifts, but this unity of family connection remains as a fixed origin as well as a centre of desire, a source of order and identity which is as much a *telos* as an *archē* in the narrative 'returns' of the plot. It is what holds together the well-known thematics of the domestic hearth and the innocent child in Dickens, though both are surface effects of a pervasive movement of return which is, I believe, a most important source of narrative bond in the novel.

It is in this respect that the integrity of the family, particularly in its essential triadic form, is affirmed by the narrative and also underpins it. I mean integrity as both moral worth and actual unity, and Lady Dedlock's tragedy is largely caused by the growing conflict between these two things. Lady Dedlock is in two families simultaneously, a natural one and a socio-legal one: the natural one has a strongly felt priority over the socio-legal one, a priority of value and of simple chronology. It came *first*. Its brief unity was the substance of that pre-narrative of which I wrote at the outset. In it Lady Dedlock is a mother and Esther finds her lost origins; it is an illegitimate family unrecognized by society and by law, founded only upon nature and 'love', a love which Dickens asserts in the strongest possible manner. At their reuniting, Esther tells us:

I raised my mother up, praying and beseeching her not to stoop before me in such affliction and humiliation. I did so in broken, incoherent words; for, besides the trouble I was in, it frightened me to see her at *my* feet. I told her—or I tried to tell her—that if it were for me, her child, under any circumstances to take upon me to forgive her, I did it, and had done it, many, many years. I told her that my heart overflowed with love for her; *that it was natural love, which nothing in the past had changed, or could change.* That it was not for me, then resting for the first time on my mother's bosom, to take her to account for having given me life; but that my duty was to bless her and receive her, though the whole world turned from her, and that I only asked her leave to do it. I held my mother in my embrace, and she held me in hers; and among the still woods in the silence of the summer day, there seemed to be nothing but our two troubled minds that was not at peace. (ch. 36; my italics)

This 'natural love', emphasized in its naturalness by its context in the still woods on a summer's day, by the young girl 'resting for the first time on my mother's bosom', not only recalls the 'natural love' and scenes of reuniting between George and his mother and Richard and Jarndyce, but indicts the frozen, deadening, *institutional* family of the Dedlocks. This latter, Dickens makes clear, is a cultural fossil, somewhat like the megalosaurus which waddles up Holborn Hill in chapter 1, and hence akin to the institutional fossil of Chancery. Centred on the dreary gloom of Chesney Wold, with its rain, ghosts, and empty corridors, the Dedlock family with its heavy emphasis on ageless tradition and aristocratic honour is a deathly, reified conception of family where all living, 'natural' relations have long ago become hard and empty forms like the unbending civility of Sir Leicester. In one sense, the Dedlocks are a straightforward symbol of a decaying class, a family network of privilege and ennui hurried into a timely grave by Dickens the busy bourgeois. When Mr Rouncewell says to George that the family is finished—'But it's breaking up, my dear; the great old Dedlock family is breaking up'—the particular tragedy of Sir Leicester and his wife is here a sad expression of a wider movement in which the aristocratic family destroys itself from within. The relations have become mere forms of scrupulous politeness, and when 'real' feeling does burst through, in the 'natural' love of Lady Dedlock repressed for so many years and the real affection which Sir Leicester had for his wife, it has a destructive force which bursts the family apart. But in another sense, the Dedlock honour is not simply a class phenomenon, tied to the disintegration of the aristocracy in the nineteenth century, but a general social phenomenon, where *family* name has replaced living relations by a desiccated line of genealogy. In one way, the Dedlocks are a great family, with vast family possessions and an unbroken lineage: in another they are no family at all, with no children, no openness, and no *connection* between people to match those of the inhabitants of Bleak House. There is nothing *natural* left to the Dedlocks which has not been buried deep beneath the dead weight of a social form, and as such 'family' is simply a name without content—or rather a name which perverts the 'true' and authentic nature of family connection rediscovered in the brief reunion of Esther with her mother. Lady Dedlock's moral dilemma is that, being in both the 'natural' family and the institutional family simultaneously, she actually belongs to neither: she cannot be a 'true' mother to Esther without harming her husband, yet she cannot continue in her role as the perfectly self-possessed aristocratic wife without violating her inner maternal feeling.

But the divided identity of Lady Dedlock is not a simple split between two equal but opposed roles. It is rather the disjunction between a latent, underlying 'reality' and a deceptive external appearance—a passionate, remorseful, natural mother beneath the artificial surface of a consciously willed disguise:

'My child, my child!' she said. 'For the last time! These kisses for the last time! These arms upon my neck for the last time! We shall meet no more. To hope to do what I seek to do, I must be what I have been so long. Such is my reward and doom. If you hear of Lady Dedlock, brilliant, prosperous, and flattered; think of your wretched mother, conscious-stricken, underneath that mask! Think that the reality is in her suffering, in her useless remorse, in her murdering within her breast the only love and truth of which it is capable!' (ch. 36).

The character of Lady Dedlock is structured on this blocked or closed opposition between a manifest appearance and a latent truth in which the 'blocking' is also a part of the truth and must be included in it. The epistemology, then, is that of *Sartor Resartus* and *Vanity Fair*, it is a clothes-philosophy, an uncomplicated model of understanding predicated upon the confident belief that beneath the falsehood, concealment, and muddle there is a solid body of truth: a clothes-philosophy 'of how society everywhere disguises social reality in an elegant carapace of social convention and social sham'. Knowledge can find its object below the surface in a systematic tracking-down of a truth that is hidden and may be found: knowledge, in other words, is the discovery of a secret, it is the opening of something inside which is 'dead-locked'. Furthermore, knowledge in this sense only establishes what is already there, the revelation of a secret is only a repetition, it repeats what already *was* simply by its recovery.

In *Bleak House* what is gradually uncovered is a network of 'true connection'. The word 'true' must be read here with both of the meanings that Dickens gives it when he talks of 'the only love and *truth*' of which Lady Dedlock is capable— that is to say 'true' in the sense of sincere and faithful affection as well as 'true' as an accurate account of reality. True connection is what binds Esther to her mother, to Tom Jarndyce, and to Alan Woodcourt; it is what binds Ada to Richard and George to Mrs Rouncewell, the Bagnets to one another and to George; it is what binds Caddy to her husband and Mr Snagsby to Jo, and what binds Lady Dedlock to her dead lover Captain Hawdon. These connections are networks of truth and of 'true connections', and it is these which constitute the basis of *understanding* (again a word to be taken in both its meanings) in the text. *Bleak House* is a description of the process of recovery of this true connection through a sentimental quest for origins which is at once nostalgic and remorseful. This 'quest for origins' returns, evidently enough, to the chaos of Chancery. The confusion of truth in Chancery, its loss beneath the plethoric over-production of documents and words, is inseparable from the breaking of bonds between people and a consequent pervasive isolation of those involved: its irony as an institution is that its ostensible function is to stabilize and settle family links which have been disrupted, it *ought* to regularize and maintain the continuity of kinship relations, though in fact it does just the opposite. What it becomes is a vast blocking mechanism, one of four such which are given a specific geographical identity, a place, in the book: Chesney Wold; Krook's rag-and-bottle shop; Tom-all-Alone's; Chancery.

These four places give a clear topological definition and separation to those forces of entropy which threaten 'true connection'. They are all spatial metaphors of various types of *discursive closure*. In a gesture which is almost a reflex, Dickens habitually expresses social forces in terms of places, and these four all operate as terminals within the immensely complex systems of information and social interrelation circulating through the novel. They block up normal communication and normal intercourse in spaces which are, in all four cases, dark, closed in, disturbed, secretive, and diseased. They are places where the open and sincere connection between people cannot exist and where the fundamental Dickensian principle of ordered truth sustained by close social bonds can no longer operate—places indeed where this latter is under a considerable threat of disintegration.

Chesney Wold and the world of fashion which adheres to it 'is not so unlike the Court of Chancery, but that we may pass from one scene to the other as the crow flies'. It is 'a deadened world, and its growth is sometimes unhealthy for want of air'. The first description of it follows all the parameters given above. It is closed in, dark, and secretive, disturbed by the wandering presence of its ghost and diseased with mould and the taint of death:

The waters are out in Lincolnshire. An arch of the bridge in the park has been sapped and sopped away. The adjacent low lying ground, for half a mile in breadth, is a stagnant river, with melancholy trees for islands in it, and a surface punctured all over, all day long, with falling rain . . . The view from my Lady Dedlock's own windows is alternately a lead-coloured view, and a view in Indian ink . . . On Sundays, the little church in the park is mouldy; the oaken pulpit breaks out into a cold sweat; and there is a general smell and taste as of the ancient Dedlocks in their graves. (ch. 2)

Although Dedlock Hall is described as slightly less moribund later on, these characteristics are repeated throughout the novel, and the closing description of it in chapter 66 recapitulates the first, perhaps the only change being that the mausoleum mentioned in chapter 2 takes on an emphasized significance in chapter 66.

With a kind of compulsive repetition which has already been identified, Chancery, the rag-and-bottle shop, and Tom-all-Alone's become, at significant moments in the novel, closed off. Chesney Wold is shuttered and silent; the pauper graveyard which is the very centre of Tom-all-Alone's is locked up, so that no living character enters its contagious precincts (though several journeys in the book have led up to its closed gates); the rag-and-bottle shop, 'foggy and dark', is locked up and shuttered after the death of Mr Krook; and Chancery, closed in the summer recess, has idleness and pensiveness hanging 'like some great veil of rust, or gigantic cobweb' (ch. 19) over the legal neighbourhood. The physical closure of these places, in clear contrast to the airy brightness of Bleak House, makes them secret and repressive. They are all labyrinthine: the maze of court-rooms and store-rooms in Chancery reflects the labyrinth of shuttered corridors at Chesney Wold, which in turn mirror the maze of chaotic rooms at Krook's and the muddle of dark alleys and tenements in Tom-all-Alone's. Chancery is a 'labyrinth of mysteries', Chesney Wold a 'labyrinth of Grandeur', Krook's is all 'dark passages and dark doors' and nothing is to be seen in Tom's but 'the crazy houses shut up and silent'.

But perhaps most important is that they are all centres of disease. Richard becomes 'infected'—the word is Dickens's own—by the blighting influence of Chancery, and Tom Jarndyce says to Esther that 'It is in the subtle poison of such abuses to breed such diseases. His blood is infected, and objects lose their natural aspects in his sight. It is not his fault' (ch. 35). The lawsuit is described by Richard's guardian as a centre of contagion: 'It is a terrible misfortune, little woman, to be ever drawn within the influence of Jarndyce and Jarndyce. I know none greater. By little and little he has been induced to trust in that rotten reed, and it communicates some portion of its rottenness to everything around him' (ch. 35).

We have already noted the mould and smell and taste of death at Chesney Wold, and the disease imagery used of Krook's shop, particularly in the famous scene of spontaneous combustion, which reaches extraordinary density. Whilst 'Weevle' (alias Tony Jobling) awaits midnight to look at the documents in Krook's possession, the tainting soot and yellow grease (all that remains of Krook!) fouls the air with smears like black fat: 'A thick yellow liquor defiles them, which is offensive to the touch and sight and more offensive to the smell. A stagnant, sickening oil, with some natural repulsion in it that makes them both shudder' (ch. 32).

Disease spreads out from these places, following the lines of information and connection which link all the narrative centres together, withering and destroying them.

The exact status of the metaphorical and real diseases which cling to certain centres of secrecy and closure in the novel is difficult to fix accurately, but in Dickens's mind it appears to be repeatedly identified with an encroaching disorder of communication and community, any kind of threat to 'normal', truthful language and close, integrated social bonds. Sickness and malignancy spread out from those places where there are secrets and mysteries cutting people off from each other and breeding mistrust and antagonisms. Disease results from, or grows to replace, those enclaves of social darkness which include the slum and the bureaucracy and the fossilized shell of the landed gentry, and which appear hostile to the Dickensian norm of sincerity and truth embodied in the parental bonds of the (bourgeois) family. It is therefore all the more fitting that when the second Bleak House is built, the new family which fills it should be that of the doctor, Allan Woodcourt, a termination of the narrative which affirms both the symbolic endurance of the Bleak House community, but also its successful opposition to the centres of disease which have surrounded it throughout the story.

Jo and Richard are innocent carriers of this disease, but the central, diseased character in the book is Tulkinghorn, the one figure to whom all the others are in some way bound. Many times, Dickens describes him as 'rusty'. When first introduced the old gentleman is 'rusty to look at'; in chapter 10, both he and his apartment are 'rusty, out-of-date'; in chapter 27 the lawyer arrives to see Mr George 'rustily dressed', and again later this burrower among secrets is called a 'rusty lawyer'. In this connection, the word rust has nothing to do with the oxidation of ferrous substance, but means both disease of plants (a canker like wheat-rust) and 'a deteriorating or impairing effect upon character and ability, especially as the result of inactivity' (*OED*). Signifying both material and moral corruption, it also has a slang meaning in the nineteenth century, meaning money, and in Mayhew's *Paved with Gold*,[2] a thief remarks that 'There's no chance of "nabbing any rust" (taking any money)' (p. 284). Interestingly enough, then, Tulkinghorn as a character exhibits exactly the same sequence of characteristics which are displayed by *places* in *Bleak House*, he is dark, closed, a centre of secrecy, refusing all sincere and open relation to others, a hoarder diseased by a canker of 'rust':

The old gentleman is rusty to look at, but is reputed to have made good thrift out of aristocratic marriage settlements and aristocratic wills, and to be very rich. He is surrounded by a mysterious halo of family confidences, of which he is known to be the silent depository. There are noble Mausoleums rooted for centuries in retired glades or parks, among the growing timber and the fern, which perhaps hold fewer noble secrets than walk abroad among men, shut up in the breast of Mr Tulkinghorn . . . One peculiarity of his black clothes, and of his black stockings, be they silk or worsted, is that they never shine. Mute, close irresponsive to any glancing light, his dress is like himself. He never converses, when not professionally consulted. (ch. 2)

The sort of need which drives Dickens to overdetermine every instance in *Bleak House* operates here as well. At the level of style, the insistent repetition of 'rusty' is a familiar type of 'nervous tic' in Dickensian characterization, whereby a repeated phrase serves to recall and fix a particular person. The counterpart of this at the level of content is Mr Vholes, surely nothing more than a reduced copy of Tulkinghorn. Vholes is 'close, buttoned-up' with a whispery voice and stifled tone, dressed like Tulkinghorn in black clothes,

[2] London, 1858.

'funeral gloves', and 'black dye from head to foot'. The drive to repeat is manifest at different levels of the text, and marks style as well as narrative. In this respect at least, the thesis of narrative structuralism which posited a certain homology between sentence structure and plot structure is correct, and we can clearly see the doubling over of the one *through* the other at work in *Bleak House*.

Tulkinghorn is a 'great reservoir of confidences', metaphorically linked with the 'stagnant river' surrounding Chesney Wold and the stagnant oil of Krook's house. The association of secrecy and disease, closure and corrosion which organizes the symbolic structuration of the text is most clearly embodied in Tulkinghorn. In the cold and relentless pursuit of his investigation he produces a plot, he is a threat, he is, of all people, against 'connection'. His accumulated power is purely destructive, it is what destroys the Dedlock family and Jo, and nearly destroys George and Esther. His self-repression and willed isolation, having neither family nor friends, contrasts strongly with the qualities of Inspector Bucket, a man who has an outstanding 'adaptability to all grades' of society, whose wife helps him in his quest, and whose brilliant interrogations take the form of a friendly solicitude, the intuitive, sympathetic understanding of those around him.

In effect, Tulkinghorn is less a character and more simply a threatening force, gradually increasing the pressure upon Lady Dedlock. His motive (protecting the family honour of Sir Leicester) is curiously contradictory in the light of the damage he knows his revelation will do, and appears to me as a superficial rationalization of his actual position in the narrative. Like Krook and Chancery, he is a hoarder of language, a man 'severely and strictly self-repressed' who, by refusing to exchange and to join, ends by destroying himself and others. He is part of an identically repeated pattern in the novel which transcends him as a character, and which always locates the subversion of knowledge and language in the same *position* as the subversion of social connection. The information he collects he keeps, not so that he may share it later on, but so that he may have the power that secrecy confers to release it in a flood with destructive force. Tulkinghorn's refusal to share and exchange his knowledge, his deliberate holding back things until they have become dangerous, indicates how far Dickens associated exchange (kinship, information) with health on the one hand and stagnation (isolation, suppression) with disease on the other. This is not to propose that the bourgeois economic ideology that 'progress' is only equated with trade, expansion, and constant exchange relates in any simple way to narrative organization in Dickens, but the opposition between free exchange and stagnation is strikingly analogous to Victorian middle-class economics. The closer one looks, the more it appears that Dickens's immense appeal to his readers, despite his scathing social criticism, has something to do with writing narratives which are elaborate metaphors for the conservation and reduplication of harmonious and strong family relations within a context of freely balanced communication and trade. The narrative *plays out* (in both senses of the word, to enact and to exhaust) the threats to this homoeostatic system which endures to re-establish itself (the founding of the second Bleak House) despite the dangers outside it.

These dangers, peculiarly enough, annihilate *themselves*. Krook's spontaneous combustion is merely the most spectacular such self-destruction, in which plausibility is sacrificed to a deeper need in Dickens to let evil die by feeding upon itself. Jarndyce and Jarndyce ends by using up its own funds and consuming itself; Lady Dedlock, whose repression to the natural family is clear, destroys herself in remorse; and Tulkinghorn is destroyed by yet another outsider, Hortense, literally an alien, dark and secretive, without family connections, whom Dickens can use without compunction to eliminate the rusty lawyer in a way which only emphasizes that destruction and evil are *external* threats to a world of true connection. It is Hortense who exhibits in a most brilliant scene the symptoms of self-repression which Dickens describes as so disquieting. Hortense, having just been publicly snubbed by Lady Dedlock, controls and forces down her passionate anger in a terrifying act of self-control: 'Her retaliation was the most singular I could have imagined. She remained perfectly still until the carriage had turned into the drive, and then, without the least discomposure of countenance, slipped off her shoes, left them on the ground, and walked deliberately in the same direction, through the wettest of the wet grass' (ch. 18).

This 'mortification' of her impulse to revenge makes her one with those other characters (and places) which token self-repression and concealment and which thereby remain beyond the sincere universe of relationships represented by the community at Bleak House (Jarndyce, Esther, Ada, and Richard before his 'infection').

What is important in *Bleak House* is the clarity with which these differences are separated and identified. The narrative is a process of revelation, through a number of secrets, of an identifiable order which is under threat from identifiable sources: that is to say, an idealized set of relationships (which fuse together the pre-Oedipal contentment of parent and child with the idealized domestic security of the bourgeois family) are endangered from without by bureaucracy, by proletarian misery, and by a reified, static aristocracy, all of which are dangerously 'diseased'. With a confidence which is simultaneously moral, economic, and aesthetic Dickens classifies the *real* and the *false* as totally separate and separable principles: human connection, sincerity, and order against disorder, stagnation, and evil, and this presupposes as its narrative possibility the clear (and it is clarity which is in question here) articulation of the difference between connection and repression of a hidden reality which withstands all pressures and which only has to be *uncovered* to be seen. There is muddle, linguistic chaos, secrecy, falsehood, and silence, but Dickens identifies and places these forms of disorder in relation to order (Esther and her perfectly regulated accounts) so that there is in the end no doubt 'where things stand' with regard to each other. It is significant in this respect that Dickens chooses to indicate Miss Flite's insane eccentricity by a confused and disordered list of categories for the names of her birds, mixing Hope and Folly with Gammon and Spinach in a way which contrasts with Dickens's own categorical separation of principles in the novel itself.

A final distinction must be made between the active subversion of normal communication and passive exclusion from it: in other words something must be said about those characters in *Bleak House* who stand *outside* language.

Of the seventy or so named characters who pass in and out of the chapters of the novel, the very last, introduced two pages from the end of the story, is Caddy Jellyby's little baby girl, born deaf and dumb. For a novel purporting to dwell upon the 'romantic side of familiar things', it appears a gratuitously unpleasant touch, a single nasty discord in what is otherwise a bland and comfortable rounding-off of the narrative by Esther, who is benignly parcelling out happy marriages, modest but adequate incomes, and healthy children. The deaf and dumb girl could have been meant as a small touch of dissonant naturalism introduced by Dickens to shake the predictable complacency of the happy ending, or it could have been a final touch of pathos—Dickens always found it difficult to resist the image of a helpless and pathetic child in his compositions—or even a simple device for emphasizing the saintly qualities of Caddy, of whom Esther remarks: 'I believe there never was a better mother than Caddy, who learns, in her scanty intervals of leisure, innumerable deaf and dumb arts, to soften the affliction of her child' (ch. 67).

A deaf and dumb child, forever outside of language and ordinary communication, only in contact with its loving mother, is an extreme type of that familiar Dickens symbol of the child-innocent.[3] But above this, the relation of the child to its mother and to language gives this handicapped girl, born and disposed of in a sentence, a tiny, distant, but significant position in the greater concerns of *Bleak House*.

---

[3] We can find the prototype of this child-innocent in the little girl, 'blind, deaf, and dumb', whom Dickens saw at the Perkins Institution in Boston and whose story he tells at some length in ch. 3 of *American Notes*. He had been deeply moved and impressed by the plight and bravery of the girl, Laura Bridgman, who, like Jo, is held up as a kind of example and sacrificial lesson to the world.

She is simply the last and perhaps the most extreme of a number of innocents in the novel who become excluded from the 'normal' world of communication only to become passive, helpless victims. Little Jo, used and hunted down, is an illiterate, and the misfortunes of Caddy Jellyby's baby girl closely recall Dickens's description of Jo as 'stone blind and dumb':

It must be a strange state to be like Jo! To shuffle through the streets, unfamiliar with the shapes, and in utter darkness as to the meaning, of those mysterious symbols, so abundant over the shops, and at the corners of the streets, and on the doors, and in the windows! To see people read, and to see people write, and to see the postmen deliver letters, and not to have the least idea of all that language—to be, to every scrap of it, stone blind and dumb! (ch. 16)

The inflammable Mr Krook is another such: like Jo he is an illiterate, and spends his time, when not chronically drunk, vainly trying to learn to read, a task which he never manages to complete to the time of his bizarre death. In the rag-and-bottle shop, that 'secret house' where he lives surrounded by letters, documents, papers, wills, testaments, a chaotic muddle of writing which he is quite unable to decipher, Krook lives a close, suspicious, drunken old man excluded from the network of messages which engulf him. And his situation is not all that different from that of Mr Jellyby, who sits in his house a broken man swamped by his wife's letters and communications, thousands upon thousands of words of misplaced and exotic philanthropy, which have inexorably taken over his house and destroyed his family. Mr Jellyby, pushed to bankruptcy and misery by his wife's rapacious benevolence, is also a mute—the most he has ever been known to utter, with tremendous effort, are three words of an uncompleted sentence. And Sir Leicester Dedlock, happily innocent of the thickening net of secrets and deceptions around him, is struck dumb on discovering the truth, again recalling Caddy Jellyby's little child. He finishes his days riding silently round his decaying estates at

Chesney Wold, able to utter words and scribble notes with immense difficulty, but hardly ever desiring to do so.

These important characters, all excluded in some way from language, bring us to the heart of a central connection in Dickens's writing between innocence, exclusion, social connectedness, and sacrifice. The suffering and death which afflict these illiterates and mutes are in no way required by the exigencies of the plot, and the striking way in which Dickens sacrifices these four people appears to derive from ulterior forces rather than local narrative necessity. It is as if the same form of latent connections which we have seen between social connection/normal communication, and between disruption/disordered communication, extended to embrace sacrifice/mutism as well. The same, recurrent link which has existed from time immemorial between *innocence* and *sacrifice* is expressed and repeated in *Bleak House*, and serves, as such sacrifice has always served, to strengthen and affirm social connection. In *Les Formes élémentaires de la vie réligieuse*, Durkheim wrote of sacrifical rites as follows: 'Les rîtes sont, avant tous, les moyens par lesquels le groupe social se réaffirme périodiquement.'[4]

It is difficult to know exactly why a sacrifice must be pure and innocent, over and above a certain fitting cleanliness of spirit which would make it acceptable to the gods, but something of the same connection is visible in Dickens's attitude to Jo, whose death conforms remarkably to the requirements of scapegoating, even to his being driven out into the wilderness by the appointed officer of the State: '"Hook it! Nobody wants you here", he ses. "You hook it. You go and tramp", he ses. "You move on", he ses. "Don't let me ever see you nowheres within forty miles of London, or you'll repent it"' (ch. 46).

Since for Dickens being excluded from language is a privileged kind of innocence, the scapegoating of Jo and the sacrifice of the others has a special aptness. If, as I have written, *Bleak House* is essentially concerned with the preserva-

---

[4] E. Durkheim, *Les Formes élémentaires de la vie réligieuse* (Paris, 1912), 553.

tion and endurance of social connectedness, it is perhaps not surprising to find sacrifice, the pathos of exclusion, operating in the narrative. It would certainly make sense of that otherwise bizarre episode, the spontaneous combustion of Krook. In what is almost a grotesque parody of a burnt offering Dickens sacrifices the illiterate drunkard not because some detail of the plot structure required him out of the way, but because, as Durkheim says, rites are above all the means by which the social group is periodically reaffirmed. Thus the deaths of Jo and Krook, and the silence of Jellyby and Sir Leicester, by being 'outside' and 'afflicted', strengthen by contrast and opposition the unity of those within. However sad and moving the plight of the mutes and illiterates in the text, their isolation, expulsion, and suffering serves to draw the ranks of those within language closer together—serves, once more, to forge social connection.

This latter exists as a kind of reduplicated space (Bleak House and its double) between three alien borders: the riotous over-production of information at Chancery and the rag-and-bottle shop; the hoarded information of Tulkinghorn and Vholes; the silence of mutism and illiteracy. Between these three the frequent drawing-room conversations of Esther, Jarndyce, and the others at Bleak House stand as a paradigm of balanced and domestic intercourse: language at home with itself. Threatened from outside by unbalanced and abnormal forms of meaning, this family conversation establishes the norm within the novel of what comfortable and felicitous community is about: it is modelled upon the idealized verbal exchange of the middle-class drawing-room.

It is only at this stage that the full complexity of narrative structure in *Bleak House* may be realized. Its process of continual repetition and recall establishes a narrative movement which is retroactive and retrospective, a turning-back to 'that pleasant country, where the old times are'. Its secrets, which proliferate in the text, tend in the same way to be a quest back to origins which are recognized and identified after having been temporarily hidden. Thus knowledge in *Bleak House* is a systematic tracking-down of concealed truth, of a reality which already exists in secret scraps and fragments and which true connection will restore to wholeness. In *Bleak House* doubt and mystery disperse as these fragments of evidence cohere. Things group themselves to reveal their identity, things 'fall into place'. The connections which emerge reveal a formalized structure which is extensive and enduring. Goodness, truth, regulated exchanges of language, family bonds—these are placed together as a contiguous and coherent order of stable existence. Evil, secrecy, disease, stagnation, malformations of language, disrupted and broken bonds—these too are placed together as a contiguous order, but in opposition to the first, attacking it and threatening disintegration. It is connection and communication which, by an iterative process of recall and remembrance, rescue order and security from danger, not by moving forward but by going back, tracking down the past and repeating it. And when it eventually emerges, this past-becomes-future is not simply the bland satisfaction of a nostalgic longing, but a most remarkably complex narrative enactment: what emerges almost unnoticed as the narrative unfolds is the proposal, definition, and consolidation of truth in a way which makes it equivalent to the Victorian middle-class ideal of family and economy. Freed from the aristocracy at Chesney Wold, the diseased poor in Tom-all-Alone's, and the bureaucrats at Chancery, truth returns to its 'origins'—to its family, and its place by the fireside—it returns to Bleak House.

5 Ironic Equivalence: A Reading of Thomas Pynchon's 'Mortality and Mercy in Vienna'

'Mortality and Mercy in Vienna' by Thomas Pynchon, first published in 1959,[1] is one of the finest short stories published since the war. It has the density, allusiveness, and breadth of a full novel without losing the shock peripeteia of the classic short story. Indeed, the 'shocking' ending and its relation to the rest of the story are most revealing about Pynchon's writing as a whole and the contradictory tradition of American liberalism from which it issues. It coerces the central liberal values of humanist sympathy, compassion, care, and concern ('Mercy') into a confrontation with violence, paranoia, and an ironic acceptance of murder ('Mortality'). Written between the end of the Korean war and the beginning of the Vietnam war, Pynchon's story exposes the bitter 'paradox' of an American liberalism which finds, time and again, that the eventual form taken by its careful concern is brutality and violence.

Siegel, a young diplomat working for an unspecified Government commission, arrives at a Washington party to discover that the host—a surprising *doppelgänger* of himself—is just leaving and that he, Siegel, is now in charge. The party degenerates, people keep coming to Siegel to confess their problems and sins and he is embarrassed and annoyed by the frequency, the forced intimacy, and above all by the content of these 'Confessionals'. But as the party accelerates to its chaotic climax, he notices that one of the guests, a displaced

First published in *Critical Quarterly*, 23 (1981).
[1] 'Mortality and Mercy in Vienna' first appeared in *Epoch*, 9 (1959). It was published in Britain by Aloes Books (London, n.d., unpaginated).

Ojibwa Indian called Irving Loon, is about to suffer from a strange attack of the 'Windigo psychosis', an aberration of his own tribal culture which, any moment now, will turn him into a frenzied cannibal. Coolly, Siegel assesses what he should do. It takes him five seconds. He tells no one. As he walks out of the party he sees the Indian making towards an automatic rifle hung on the wall, and by the time he gets into the street he hears the first burst of fire and the first screams of the party-goers.

The question is: was Siegel's decision the result of a spiritual logic built up in hints and scraps throughout the story, or was it 'loony' (as the name Irving Loon suggests), a further bit of chaotic, anarchistic madness which simply pushed the breakdown and degeneracy of the party to its own logical point of self-destruction?

The story itself proposes and balances both possibilities. 'Mortality and Mercy' resembles in this Pynchon's earlier story 'Entropy', but also prefigures important aspects of *The Crying of Lot 49*, *V*, and *Gravity's Rainbow*. It plots a doubleness where the loonies look grimly sane, and the sane world looks like an asylum, or nightmare, or a chaotic party. Pynchon characters generally have some cosmic system which sometimes looks like a cybernetic theory, sometimes like the Book of Revelation—and yet the closer we get to the rationality of the cosmic system, the more it tends to dissolve into the grotesque, the paranoid, and, in *this* story, the psychotic. Pynchon protagonists possess the unusual quality of being laconic obsessives. They move from the flip and the wry to metaphysical horror with elusive facility. Callisto, Irving Loon, Siegel, Oedipa Maas, Stencil, they all follow a trail which is like following a crazy paving to apocalypse. A trail which is either nuts and leading to paranoia and psychosis, or a trail which is the logical and sane revelation of some immense truth of an almost religious or mystical kind. The text is built upon this unknown, and the reader is held in a bizarre, fascinating narrative space, the singular quality of which is to make a radical identification of the forms of insanity and the forms of reason.

The title of the story is taken from *Measure for Measure*, and it is worth quoting the end of the Duke's speech in Act I, Scene i where the phrase occurs:

> Spirits are not finely touch'd
> But to fine issues; nor nature never lends
> The smallest scruple of her excellence
> But, like a thrifty goddess, she determines
> Herself the glory of a creditor,
> Both thanks and use. But I do bend my speech
> To one that can my part in him advertise:
> Hold therefore, Angelo.
> In our remove, be thou at full ourself
> Mortality and Mercy in Vienna
> Live in thy tongue and heart.   (lines 35–45)

Francis Douce in his *Illustrations of Shakespeare* (1807) gives us a gloss on the sentence 'Mortality and Mercy in Vienna live in thy tongue and heart', which reads: 'I delegate to thy tongue the power of pronouncing sentence of death, and to thy heart the privilege of exercising mercy.'[2] This is the charge which the old Duke puts upon Angelo, a sort of civic cleaning-up campaign to stamp out the corruption and vice to which he feels Vienna to have degenerated. We are familiar with the range of problems which arise in *Measure for Measure* when Angelo elides these two opposed powers granted him by the Duke: when Angelo *equates* 'the power of pronouncing sentence of death' with 'the privilege of exercising mercy'. The problematical disquiet of Shakespeare's play arises from the brutally forced identification of mortality with mercy, murder with forgiveness. In the sequence of actions in *Measure for Measure*, death is substituted for mercy and mercy for death so often that they appear to take on a sort of cold equivalence which calls everything into doubt. The profundity of this perverse equalling of mercy and murder is striking. If mercy equals murder, if the act of love and forgiveness is made somehow equivalent to the *crime* of murder, then all judgement is subverted. The ideas

---

[2] F. Douce, *Illustrations of Shakespeare* (1807), i. 120–1.

of law, value, and judgement are radically perverted in a universe where mortality *is* mercy. Anything goes, and it's no longer possible to judge. It is this sinister world which Angelo creates and which the end of the play, with the Duke's intervention, fails hopelessly to compensate for and correct: we are left with the pessimism of the primal identification.

Pynchon's story subverts its Shakespearean source whilst retaining a marvellous fidelity to the disturbing Jacobean equation at its heart. The obvious parallel to the Duke delegating responsibility to Angelo in *Measure for Measure* is Lupescu's delegation of the party to Siegel. And the parallel is emphasized by the name itself. 'Siegel' is the German word for 'seal' or 'impression' and this takes up the 'stamp/seal' image of *Measure for Measure*, and directly recalls the ducal stamp on the seal of commission which the Duke gives to Angelo at the beginning of the play. The power delegated by Lupescu to Siegel at the beginning of the party recalls the word-play of the Duke's first speech:

> I say, bid come before us Angelo.
> What figure of us, think you, he will bear?
> For you must know, we have with special soul
> Elected him our absence to supply;
> *Lent him our terror, drest him with our love . . .*
>
> (lines 15–19; my italics)

The oxymoron of that last line 'lent him our terror, drest him with our love', not only applies to the double qualities Lupescu bequeaths Siegel, but it begins to constitute *the* basic narrative structure of the story itself. 'Mortality and Mercy in Vienna' is a narrative oxymoron where mutually exclusive opposites are forced into a close, ironic identification (like the very title of Pynchon's novel *Gravity's Rainbow*).

Thus the host of the party is called David Lupescu. 'David' is the Saviour, the shepherd, and the Christian symbolism of the pastor and his flock is invoked throughout. Siegel thinks: 'It was a slow process and dangerous because in the course of things it was very possible to destroy not only yourself but your flock as well. He took her hand. "Come on", he said. "I'd like to meet Irving. Say for your penance ten Hail Marys and make a good Act of Contrition."' But although 'David' is the shepherd, Lupescu is a Romanian word meaning 'wolfish' (Lupescu is a Romanian). David Lupescu is both shepherd and wolf, both guardian and destroyer of the flock. He is also (and also is not) the Host. When he runs out, he says to Siegel: "'It's all yours . . . You are now the host. As host you are a trinity. (*a*) receiver of guests"—ticking them off on his fingers— "(*b*) an enemy and (*c*) an outward manifestation for *them* of the divine body and blood."' But by the end of the story, the guests have become the host, literally the body and the blood. As he leaves the impending mayhem, Siegel thinks that 'this kind of penance was as good as any other; it was just unfortunate that Irving Loon, would be the only one partaking of any body and blood, divine or otherwise'.

It is as though the pastor had turned upon his flock and devoured it. Pynchon's eucharistic pun, which makes the host the guest, is paralleled by the ecumenical *rapprochement* of Jew and Jesuit in Siegel. Born of Jewish father and Catholic mother, these two warring factions within him (remember Grossmann's taunt at College: "'It is the seed of your destruction", he would murmur. "House divided against itself?"') the warring factions are by the end of the story resolved into a sort of paradoxical equivalence:

He [Siegel] figured there were about sixty seconds to make a decision, and now the still small Jesuit voice, realising that the miracle *was* in his hands after all, for real, vaunted with the same sense of exhilaration Siegel had once felt seeing five hundred hysterical freshmen advancing on the women's dorms, knowing it was he who had set it all in motion. And the other, gentle part of him sang *kaddishes* for the dead and mourned over the Jesuit's happiness, realising however that this kind of penance was as good as any other . . . It took no more than five seconds for the two sides to agree that there was really only one course to take.

Again, Pynchon has created a type of oxymoron whereby the active, manœuvring Jesuit and the melancholy Jew become the same voice.

Terms which under ordinary circumstances are mutually exclusive are forced into a kind of identity where the one becomes a version of the other. The form is rather like a metaphor in which we cannot see which is the vehicle and which the tenor—there is no one referential set which controls the narrative: salvation *is* destruction; order *is* chaos; justice *is* psychosis; mercy *is* mortality. When Siegel sees what is going to happen, Pynchon writes, 'Siegel had the power to work for these parishioners a kind of miracle, to bring them a very tangible salvation. A miracle involving a host, true, but like no holy Eucharist.' This identification of the Christian mythic pattern of salvation and redemption with clinical psychosis is not a simple undermining of God by Freud. Siegel sees himself in the religious terminology of prophet and healer rather than the modern psychoanalytic counterpart of doctor and fortune-teller. Indeed Pynchon uses the terms of clinical psychiatry in his stories, but his analysts, like Geronimo Diaz in *Lowlands* and Dr Hilarius in *The Crying of Lot 49* are usually raving mad. Once more, the oxymoron of terms is employed, and in both of those stories the patient becomes the analyst and vice versa, even though both also stay in their original roles. Thus the narrative operates to suspend interpretation and to fox judgement. The domestic suddenly gapes open and becomes the cosmic; a rather over-indulgent, slightly chaotic Washington party in the 1950s suddenly becomes the heart of darkness, a nightmare of evil. The mundane only has to flicker a little and it arches out into hysterical instability: a wry word in the bedroom is made to appear, in the next sentence, like a metaphysical indictment.

Debbie Considine's involved, messy story of the infidelity and bitching of the people at the party is at once an ironic parody of American divorce/partner-swapping culture and also the revelation of some universal moral infection. The story is given twice, once as situation comedy, the second time as a Joseph Conrad nightmare, and this forcing of the one through the other is a formal as well as material figure in the text—mystical overwriting and comic understatement are not simply juxtaposed but compressed by a switching mechanism which reveals them to be the positive and negative of the same pulse.

On the one hand Pynchon has a profoundly pessimistic reading of culture and his use of entropic degeneration has been frequently noted. He is almost Spenglerian in his gloom about the decadence of modern social life. In 'Entropy', the short story written about two years[3] before 'Mortality and Mercy', Callistro, the protagonist, is writing his autobiography:

'Nevertheless', continued Callistro, 'he found in entropy or the measure of disorganization for a closed system an adequate metaphor to apply to certain phenomena in his own world. He saw, for example, the younger generation responding to Madison Avenue with the same spleen he had once reserved for Wall Street, and in American 'Consumerism' discovered a similar tendency from the least to the most probable, from differentiation to sameness from ordered individuality to a kind of chaos. He found himself, in short, restating Gibbs' prediction in social terms, and envisioned a heat-death for his culture in which ideas, like heat-energy, would no longer be transferred, since each point in it would ultimately have the same quantity of energy.' (*Slow Learner*, 88–9)

This indicates Pynchon's obsession with the entropic model of the world in which everything tends by a law of physics towards chaos and degeneration. It also gives us a gloss on the suddenly very grim, nihilistic thoughts which Siegel has at the end of the party, when once again he borrows from Conrad's *Heart of Darkness*:

Lupescu . . . really had, like some Kurtz, been possessed by the heart of a darkness in which no ivory was ever sent out from the interior, but instead hoarded jealously by each of its gatherers to build painfully, fragment by fragment, temples to the glory of some imago or obsession, and decorated inside with the art work of dream and nightmare, and locked finally against a hostile forest, each 'agent' his own ivory tower, having no windows to look out

---

[3] 'Entropy' first appeared in the *Kenyon Review*, 22 (1960); it is published in Britain in the collection of Pynchon's early stories, *Slow Learner* (London, 1985).

of, turning further and further inward and cherishing a small flame behind the altar.

There is real bitterness in these lines. Solipsism, resulting from the extension of a hedonistic consumer culture, is for Pynchon a nightmare of decadence. Many of his characters are, in various ways, pigs. Pig Bodine recurs through his novels; Harvey Duckworth comes in carrying his girl piggy-back, there is Sam Fleischmann, Meatball Mulligan, Krinkles Porcino, and the symbol which hangs over the whole party, the pig's foetus which Lupescu hangs up at the beginning of the evening, when he says: 'Tonight. Of course. Why. Why not. Pig foetus. Symbol. God, what a symbol.'

The pig foetus suspended above the party has been put there by Lupescu in imitation of one used at a 'Dada exhibit in Paris on Christmas eve, 1919'. As such it infects the party with its own grotesque symbolism and foregrounds the surrealist dislocation of the story, what Siegal later calls 'this whole absurd surrealist atmosphere'. But the foetus is also an evident part of Pynchon's wider use of piggy animalism in this and other works. The stronger symbolic resonance of the pig characters and the pig foetus suspended above them recalls the inherent iconic tradition which relates pigs to the inseparableness of sinful excess and sacrifice. In the Bestiaries[4] the pig is said to signify 'Sinners and unclean persons or heretics; penitents who have become slack and have an eye for those sins which they have wept for, unclean and wanton men or spirits; foul thoughts and fleshly lusts from which proceed unproductive works, as though boiled away.'

This seems an accurate moralistic summary of Lupescu's friends at the party, and taken in conjunction with the series of confessions which constitute the ironic and degenerating religious lineaments of the plot, indexes the deeper connection between Pynchon's porcine preoccupations and the narrative itself—the murderous sacrifice of sinners which is also an act of mercy. This ironic equivalence is a central feature of the iconic tradition of the pig—particularly the Jacobean,

---

[4] See F. C. Sillar and R. M. Meyler, *The Symbolic Pig* (Edinburgh, 1961), 21.

which recurs endlessly in Pynchon's novels and relates back to the Shakespearean title of this story. In his fascinating book on literary metamorphosis, *The Gaping Pig*,[5] Irving Massey writes of the 'Elizabethan–Jacobean preoccupation with the pig caught in the open-mouthed squeal':

The image produces the kind of uninterpretable paradox that is characteristic of metamorphosis. Is it a mockery of human laughter? Is it the agonized shriek of the animal? Laughter or desperation? A hideous expression of life, or the frozen face of death? In either case, it seems to belong to that metamorphic world that persistently ridicules our attempts at interpretation. (pp. 11–12)

This seems to me perfectly apposite for Pynchon's use of the foetus and the ambiguous symbolic centre which it forms to his story. The filth, the chaos, the greed, the bloated, piggy self-centredness of the party-goers run as a leitmotif throughout, and lead, insistently, to that side of Pynchon which wants to 'exterminate all the brutes'. Like Angelo, who decreed death as a solution to the festering flesh-pots of corrupt Vienna, Siegel, Lupescu, and Irving Loon are powerfully attracted by terrorism; Lupescu, like the Duke, 'lends Siegel his terror'. And there may be more than accident in the pun of Siegel's name, 'Sieg Heil'—and the reference to Vienna in the title may have as much to do with the birthplace of national socialism as with its Shakespearean source. Again one is caught: between a hinted parody of fascism and the gleaming desire for the final solution, the pure terror of Jacobean revenge. 'For the things that rule Irving Loon, the concentration of obscure cosmic forces . . . cynical terrorists, savage and amoral deities.'

Eliot's *Waste Land* and Conrad's *Heart of Darkness*, in addition to *Measure for Measure*, lie behind and in the story. T. S. Eliot's elegiac lament for the loss of spiritual vitality in modern city culture is caricatured in Debbie Considine's sentimental description of Irving Loon:

He hasn't spoken a word for two days. I feel . . . that it's not only nostalgia for the wilderness, but almost as if somehow out there, in

[5] California, 1976.

the hinterlands with nothing but snow and forests and a few beavers and moose, he has come close to something which city dwellers never find all their lives, may never even be aware exists, and it's this that he misses, that the city kills or hides from him. I'll be damned thought Siegel. This broad is serious.

Irving is made the instrument of revenge on a spiritually desolate social group, and it is this as much as the vengeance of the exploited cultural minority—the Jew, the Ojibwa—which is in question. The story cannot be read simply as anti-imperialist, though the inset narrative about Grossmann is important. In Grossmann's gradual succumbing to East Coast cosmopolitanism we get a parallel to the sad story of Irving Loon, and a further index of Pynchon's preoccupation with the proliferating bourgeois culture which Siegel, at least, detests.

What interests me in the story though is not so much the relatively overt passages of critique as the political occlusion of the messianic and the domestic. The text does not simply 'hesitate' between opposed routes, salvation or psychosis, indeed, we're never really offered the choice. What it does is make us uncertain whether we're at a Washington party or on the eve of apocalypse.

We do not wait *eagerly to know*, for the mode of presentation is what we might call *ironic nihilist*: 'He shrugged. What the hell, stranger things had happened in Washington.' The horror of the black comedy is caught not in the extermination but in that shrug.

Any political critique of Pynchon should begin there: the shrugging-off of murder. For when the solution or resolution is a spiralling identification of madness and religion, unable to prise apart mortality and mercy, the identification is not *neutral*—however full of 'modernist' suspensions it might seem to be. Like Francis Ford Coppola's *Apocalypse Now*, which ideologically it so closely resembles, Pynchon's story dissolves its revulsion and guilt about modern America into literary analogues and stylish paradox. It is an attempt to escape through the use of neutral formal equivalence, ironic

equations of good and evil, and mythical and symbolic counterpoint. In fact, however, these devices only serve to make
the helplessness of an ensnared liberalism all the more trans-
parent. The poignancy of 'Mortality and Mercy in Vienna' is
revealed in that shrug, which is the real centre to the story. It
indexes perfectly an inability and unwillingness to intervene
in a world in which the traditional liberal humanist values
have collapsed, a world in which mercy and mortality appear
inseparable, and terrorism a kind of unfathomable justice.
The shrug shows up the fine limits of Pynchon's story at the
same time as revealing the moment (so often repeated in
recent American history) when America's confused liberalism
emerges as scandalously self-conscious indifference.

6 'The Dismal Sacred Word': Academic Language and the Social Reproduction of Seriousness

sēr´ious, a. **1.** Thoughtful, earnest, sober, sedate, responsible, not frivolous or reckless or given to trifling, (*has a ~ look, air; a ~ young person; ~ politician*, who gives his best energies to politics; *~ thought*, real deliberation). **2.** Important, demanding consideration, not to be trifled with, not slight, (*this is a ~ matter, question . . .*)

The language of most speech communities is stratified into 'high' and 'low' language. That is to say, there is a hierarchy of discourse which operates to distinguish certain language users from others on the basis of prestige and power. The 'high' language is normally associated with the most powerful socio-economic group existing at the felt centre of cultural power, and this language is mediated through institutions of education, religion, politics, and communications. The 'low' languages on the other hand are normally associated with the weakest socio-economic groups having limited control of dominant cultural agencies. Manual workers, women, adolescents, children, ethnic minorities, subcultures, and rural regions remote from the main centres all operate to a greater or lesser extent with 'low' languages in this sense.

There has recently been a spate of work, especially in France, which has begun to analyse the role of education in the process of political and cultural centralization.[1] Schools colleges, universities, and scholarship generally play a key

First published in LTP: Journal of Literature Teaching Politics, 2 (1983).

[1] See P. Achard, 'History and the Politics of Language in France', *History Workshop*, 10 (1980).

role in establishing and reproducing the high prestige language and the values embedded in it. The harnessing of a politics of language to a politics of centralization has been studied in the realms of school grammars, orthography, and literary textbooks by Renée Balibar, André Chenal, and others. Pierre Bourdieu's work on the political formation of 'taste' is a brilliant study of how aesthetic values are produced in and by the dominant language and its institutions.[2] In this country Tony Davies's work on the production of English as a discipline, Brian Street's on the politics of literacy, and the Centre for Cultural Studies' book on *Unpopular Education* follow similar lines.[3] All see education as a mechanism whereby a prestige language simultaneously canonizes itself, regularizes and endorses its system and boundaries, makes itself teachable and assimilable, and above all 'naturalizes' itself over against all competing sociolects, dialects, and registers.

The university institution of English literature is clearly a reproducer of high language in this sense. It is something which takes place on several planes at once: in the national reproduction of the 'canon'; in the academic language of literary criticism itself; and in the day-to-day routines of the classroom over against the informal languages of students. If the present-day literary academy operates with a tolerant Standard English, it also firmly places non-standard forms as less serious and less important than itself. The basic tool-kit of grammars, dictionaries, treatises on style, and so on is not only written *in* Standard English, but is the very instrument whereby Standard English is maintained, reproduced, and disseminated as authoritative. Thus in a well-known article in *Word* the sociolinguist Charles Ferguson noted (without, however, perceiving the full political implications of his observation) that high language produces a written, scholarly corpus about its own language forms and also produces a written,

---

[2] See P. Bourdieu and J.-C. Passeron, *Reproduction in Education, Society and Culture*, trans. R. Nice (London, 1977).

[3] See T. Davies, 'Education, Ideology and Literature', *Red Letters*, 7 (1978); B. Street, 'Literacy and Ideology', *Red Letters*, 12 (1982); Centre for Contemporary Cultural Studies, *Unpopular Education* (London, 1981).

scholarly corpus about the forms of the low languages:

> there is a strong tradition of grammatical study of the High form of the language. There are grammars, dictionaries, treatises on pronunciation, style, and so on. There is an established norm for pronunciation, grammar and vocabulary which allows variation only within certain limits. The orthography is well established and has little variation. By contrast, descriptive and normative studies of the Low form are either non-existent or relatively recent and slight in quantity. Often they have been carried out first or chiefly by scholars OUTSIDE the speech community and are written in other languages.[4]

Even in the dictionary it is clear that words are used and placed by a specific intention. To see a word listed alphabetically with its different meanings laid out side by side is to see it serialized for pedagogy. Uniquely, the word in a dictionary is laid out with all its meanings in a way it will never experience again in any other linguistic context, and this establishes the dictionary as a specific kind of language environment which empties the word out in a peculiar fashion. Of course, this is not to criticize dictionaries as such, it is merely to emphasize that even in a word-list the word is given a style, imbued with a specific profile under the lexicographer's hand.

This stylistic profile is inseparable from ideological context. The dictionary embodies an implicit hierarchy of language and produces a linguistic environment which, taken together, powerfully establish the high language over against all other registers, dialects, and sociolects. Let us take an example at random from *Chambers Dictionary*:

> **clapper,** (esp. in Devon) a rude bridge of slabs or planks laid across supports (dial.): a raised footpath (dial.): a rabbit-hole (obs.) (L.L. *claperium*, heap of stones, rabbit-hole).

Dictionaries are dictators with a strange way with words. The discursive context of the word here (by which I mean the total dictionary entry) is so estranging, so bizarre, that it corresponds to the Russian formalist notion of 'making-

---

[4] C. Ferguson, 'Diglossia', *Word*, 15 (1959).

strange'. Here, the word 'clapper' is taken charge of by a linguistic context so utterly different from itself that the result
is almost convulsive. The clash of dialect, sociolect, and register between the word defined and the defining words makes
the whole thing into a strained hybrid, an estrangement of
the word from its habitus and use. 'Clapper' is revealed here
as a defeated word. The entry is a revelation of hierarchy, a
placing of Devon dialect by a victorious South of England
now become 'Standard'. Somewhere along the line 'clapper'
lost out to 'rude bridge', 'raised footpath', and 'rabbit-hole'
such that it is now defined by them in a way that it can
never define them. Placed as it is, 'clapper' is given a profile
here in *Chambers Dictionary* (and *only* in the dictionary)
which is quite different from the profile it would have in its
rural Devon dialect and registers of farming, gamekeeping,
and poaching. Here the word struggles nakedly and unsuc-
cessfully against a victorious dialect (South of England), a
victorious register (university scholarship, 'book-learning'),
and a victorious sociolect (urban middle class). The words in
the dictionary find themselves struggling amidst alien words.
Strangely, by trying to grasp the word as an isolated term in
order to reveal its meanings, the dictionary gives it a feel and
a shape upon the page that it never has elsewhere. It creates
a new compound of high and low language unique in the
everyday speech habits of the community. Thus when 'clapper' is displayed alongside its etymological derivation, L.L.
claperium, the result only further distances the word from its
conventional habitus in rural Devon. The social 'origin' of
the word is replaced by a philological origin which only further estranges it from itself. It becomes a word-for-scholars,
its use value is visibly transformed by the philological orientation of its new context. 'Clapper' ceases to become the
local name for a bridge and becomes instead an *interesting
word*.

In the dictionary words are retextured and cleaned up
under the genial eye of scholarly linguistic patronage. All
words subtly modulate their meaning according to their context and a lexicon is a context like any other, it is not—as it

promises to be—*above* context. Thus in a dictionary words are revealed in all their meanings at once and this suspends the elementary semantic rule of selection and framing. The result is like a relentlessly serious process of punning, a vast assembly of humourless homonyms. This is because a key rule of dictionary-making is inclusiveness whereas a key rule of natural language use is exclusiveness. By juxtaposing all the different meanings of a given word the normal rule of meaning-making is suspended in anticipation of a future act of selection by the implicit user of the dictionary. Engorged with a surfeit of meaning, the words remain prone and immobile in a way not encountered elsewhere. This is not fanciful play: dictionaries appear to be above specific language use, they offer a simple list of 'objective' meanings, apparently immune from the pressure of context, social use, and local ideological colouring. On the contrary, the dictionary is a concrete instance of language use which imparts to each of the words in it a certain profile, a certain taste which they acquire only between its covers. The dictionary is in fact a highly idiosyncratic linguistic environment providing a word-context on the sensitive threshold of high and low forms. Whatever the humble aspiration of its makers, it functions to situate and hierarchize words in such a way that the implicit system actively *produces* the difference between high and low. It does not simply reflect an existent state of affairs, it is a central agent in bringing about that state of affairs.

Significantly, the very first English dictionary, Robert Cawdrey's *A Table Alphabeticall* (1604) was produced specifically with women and 'any other unskilfull persons' in mind. On the title-page of the small octavo volume there is the following inscription:

A Table Alphabeticall, conteyning and teaching the true writing, and understanding of hard usuall English wordes, borrowed from the Hebrew, Greeke, Latine, or French, &c. With the interpretation thereof by plain English words, gathered for the benefit & helpe of Ladies, Gentlewomen, or any other unskilfull persons.

Whereby they may the more easilie and better understand many hard English wordes, which they shall heare or read in Scriptures,

Sermons, or elsewhere, and also be made able to use the same aptly themselves.

The double movement of instruction, which preserves the hierarchy of discourse in the very act of apparently trying to abolish it, is clearly revealed in this preface to the first English dictionary. Holding out the tantalizing promise to the reader that she will gain skill and power through the purchase of the book, it nevertheless places her precisely as an outsider to her own national language, by and in the very act of producing the 'table alphabeticall'. These words are not *her* words, they belong to others, the learned men who *constitute themselves as learned* by producing the separation of language assumed and reproduced in dictionary-making. Teaching needs ignorance and the ignorant as the precondition for its own existence, and can produce it by formalizing the prestige language and making entry into that formalization a condition of social advancement. The borrowing of hard words from Hebrew and the classics not only ensures the authority of religious and classical learning (the institutions of which excluded women completely until very recently), it produces an exclusive lexicon for the high language generally which, codified and systematized in dictionaries, reproduces and objectifies its authority too (and even today the frequency of use of latinate terms is a clear indicator of sociolect).

For a long period in the early history of dictionary-making the lexicographer's art was seen to consist in listing and defining what were termed 'hard words'. Edmund Coote in his *English Schoole-Maister* (1596) teaches how 'any unskilfull person' may understand 'hard English words' (title-page); John Bullokar teachers the interpretation of 'the hardest words used in our Language' (*An English Expositor*, 1616, title-page); Cockeram's *English Dictionarie* (1623) is defined on its title-page as 'An Interpreter of hard English Words', and the phrase itself persists up to the present. These 'hard words' were in fact largely Latin words used in high discourses of religion and book-learning. However, the association established between dictionaries, difficulty and an arduous seriousness, was thereby established at the very outset of English dictionary-making. Almost every dictionary writer (with the significant exception of John Wesley) has tended to emphasize both the seriousness and difficulty of the task itself and the high seriousness of the matter in hand. From Bullokar's remark in 1616 that 'in my younger yeares (compiling this dictionary) hath cost mee some observation, reading, study, and charge' ('To the Courteous Reader', in *An English Expositor*) to the epic account of Murray's work on the *OED* given in the biography *Caught in the Web of Words* (New Haven, Conn., 1977), lexicographers have been a model of scholarly dedication to serious learning. Murray complained that his task was almost incompatible with family life, and remarked that dictionary-making was the vocation of celibates. This is not a superficial or accidental association of lexicon with seriousness.

Seriousness always has more to do with power than with content. The authority to designate what is to be taken seriously (and the authority to enforce reverential solemnity in certain contexts) is a way of creating and maintaining power. Samuel Johnson's occasional jokes in his dictionary, and in particular the definition of himself (the lexicographer) as 'a harmless drudge', play upon the transgression of the rule of solemnity in dictionaries themselves. The authors of *A New Universal English Dictionary* (1755) remark that 'our chief Ambition has been to advance the Truth and not to amuse our Readers with *historic Romance*, and *scholastic Jargon*'.[5]

And yet, interestingly, there has been a whole other history of dictionary-making to do with low languages, where this Spirit of Gravity has been singularly absent. Starting even earlier than Cawdrey there has been a long tradition of glossaries and dictionaries of the low language which until at least 1785 general English dictionaries excluded. Talking of the first two hundred years of lexicography, Starnes and Noyes, in *The English Dictionary from Cawdrey to Johnson*,

---

[5] Noted in D. T. Starnes and G. E. Noyes, *The English Dictionary from Cawdrey to Johnson* (Chapel Hill, NC, 1946), 181.

point out that 'Despite the variety of their materials, however, none of these lexicographers showed any interest in cant, the language of rogues and vagabonds, which had won and held great popularity in literature from early Elizabethan days' (p. 212).

From Thomas Harman's glossary of cant terms, *Caveat or Warening, for Common Cursetors Vulgarely Called Vagabondes* (1567?), up to the current *Dictionary of Slang* the lexicon of low language has had an entirely different tone and style in its dictionary representations. These works correspond precisely to Ferguson's description given above, in which he describes 'normative studies of the Low form . . . carried out first or chiefly by scholars OUTSIDE the speech community and . . . written in other languages'. The point of interest is not the commonplace idea that the dominant languages dominate, but rather how the difference is inaugurated and maintained in educational institutions of language. In the separation of high and low, 'high' is defined as serious and difficult whilst 'low' is usually defined as comic and easy. It is remarkable to compare Cawdrey's preface about 'hard words' with Harman's *Caveat*. Harman introduces his glossary with the words:

Here I set before the good Reader the leud, lousey language of these lewtering Luskes *and* lasy Lorrels, where with they bye and sell the common people as they pas through the countrey. Whych language they terme Peddelars Frenche, a unknowen toung onely, but to these bold, beastly, bawdy Beggers, and vaine Vagabondes . . .[6]

That Harman's interest in low language was not unconnected with social control can be seen by the enthusiasm with which he compiled a list of his linguistic informants and then sent it off to the local magistrate, who subsequently arrested them! Most of the dictionaries of cant had similar aims. Elisha Coles wrote in the preface to his *English Dictionary* (1676): ''Tis no Disparagement to understand the Canting Terms: It may chance to save your Throat from being cut, or (at least) your Pocket from being pickt.'

[6] Early English Text Society, Extra Series, ix (1869), 82.

The very term 'cant', however, needs looking at. The language or 'anti-language' of criminal subcultures could never be clearly identified or defined from outside. Part of its function was precisely its resistance to any comprehension by the high language. On all sides it merges with slang, dialect, urban, and rural working-class sociolects, the registers of sailors, soldiers, publicans, prostitutes, market-traders, and oral folk culture generally. Many of the dictionaries of cant are notable for their strange mishmash of contents and this is not surprising given the radical heterogeneity and elusiveness of the low language itself. In contrast to the striking uniformity of the 'hard words' of academic, Latinate English, the lexicon of low language tended to be patchy and heterodox. And yet of course there is no objective sense in which these low terms are any less 'difficult', 'arduous', or 'serious', either to compile or in their content, than the lexical set *defined* as serious by the high language. Indeed, as Coles himself admits, life itself hangs on the difference. What in fact is happening in this distinction between two kinds of language is the creation of a hierarchy by the high language such that seriousness—what is to be taken seriously—is defined, literally, *in its own words*. These dictionaries encoded in their very form a decisive ideological manœuvre: they installed, in the very heart of language, not only a distinction on the grounds of seriousness but the very principle of seriousness itself. Words and things in themselves are neither serious nor comic, but the ability, the power, to legislate what shall be deemed serious is a key to hegemonic control.

It might be thought that when dictionaries became more inclusive and thorough in the nineteenth century, this polarization of high and low, serious and comic, would be absorbed within a large, 'neutral' vocabulary list. Not a bit of it. Professor N. F. Blake's *Non-Standard Language in English Literature*, published by the Language Library, reproduces the same hierarchy, the same distinction, that serious equals high language and comic equals low language. The book tells us that 'Regional varieties, cant and slang have all played their part in accentuating extremes of character or providing light relief in drama, poetry and fiction.'[7] It is not that Professor Blake is insensitive to the misrepresentation of non-standard English in the literary canon. Nor is he sympathetic to the use of non-standard for comic victimization of the unsophisticated. But in reproducing the literary canon's *own* distinction between the serious and the comic he fails to see that the 'serious' itself is being constructed through that very distinction. He says in his introduction: 'Those writers interested in comedy will increase the number of misunderstandings that can arise from this use of two languages . . . Non-standard language will therefore often signal comedy, because the serious matters will be handled by the major characters' (p. 13). But this is completely backwards. It is not that non-standard equals comedy *because* the serious matters will be handled by the major characters. What is serious and what is comic, what is 'major' and what is 'minor' is a function of the social reproduction of seriousness, itself achieved through the equation of humour with non-standard English. What needs investigation (and is sketched in a programmatic way here) is how this complex process has operated historically. Since Professor Blake looks at the matter with binoculars, one lens of which is the established literary canon, the other lens of which is the undisturbed milieu of Standard English, he cannot but reproduce the terms and definitions of 'serious' and 'comic' constructed within the literary corpus of high culture. It is precisely in the reactionary critical notion of 'comic relief' provided by 'minor characters' that the dominant culture has effected, represented, and transmitted this definition.

The social reproduction of seriousness is a key process in education. It has often been pointed out that in school what a child learns most thoroughly is not a given set of 'subjects' (French, mathematics, etc.) but subordination to a timetable and a work regime. The grid of this 'hidden' curriculum inculcates a time-consciousness which fits the child to the

---

[7] N. F. Blake, *Non-Standard Language in English Literature* (London, 1981). White's article gives no page-reference for this sentence, which we have been unable to find in Blake's book, and which may perhaps be quoted from the dust-jacket.

needs of 'clocking on' and 'clocking off'. Though this is true, there is an even earlier process of socialization at school inscribed in the architectural division of schools into playground and classroom. Through this division, the child is taught to separate the playful from the serious, and this act of division is an absolute pre-condition of present pedagogic practice. The playground is the site of a rich, varied childhood culture. In *The Lore and Language of School Children*,[8] Iona and Peter Opie have shown how a vast repertoire of chants, songs, jokes, games, riddles, and rituals saturate the open space of the playground. Easy to romanticize (the playground is also the site of bullying and displaced abjection), the playground is nevertheless the site of the 'carnivalesque', to use Mikhail Bakhtin's term. From the outset, the modern school system is predicated upon the enclosing and exclusion of the carnivalesque from its territory. The serious act of growing up and acquiring knowledge begins by inculcating the child with a primary law of double exclusion: where knowledge is, play is not; where play is, knowledge is not. The provision of playgrounds in school puts games, exuberant bodies, scatology, sexual exploration, dirt, jokes, and pleasure in an open enclave where they cannot contaminate the realm of 'pure' knowledge. Quite literally, a whole gamut of social activities and oral culture is left outside the classroom and it is this process, like that of dictionary-making, which socially reproduces seriousness and hence functions as a primary form of social control. It is striking to notice the similarities between children's language and culture as explored by the Opies, and the language and culture of other so-called 'rogues' in the cant dictionaries. In Richard Head's *Canting Academy* of 1673 we find, according to Starnes and Noyes, 'the oath taken by rogues, canting songs, "the vicious and remarkable lives of Mother Craftsby and Mrs. Wheedle," some "joviall paradoxes", songs and catches composed by "the choicest Wits of the Age," and some horrible "examples of covetousness, Idleness, Gluttony, and Lechery"' (pp. 218–19). The Opies talk

[8] Oxford, 1959.

about oaths, tangletalk, and nonsense rhymes, tongue-twisters and tales that never end, riddles, jeers, crooked answers, tricks, tricksters, and embarrassers, Greedy-guts, Lazybones, Fatties, Lankies, and improper songs. What is in question is not some nostalgic plea that these things should be 'allowed' into the classroom. There is no more sense in that than in making some archival plea for the survival of dialects. What is in question is the alignment of knowledge and power rooted in the opposition between serious and comic.

The playground/classroom division is not simply the physical and temporal separation of work and play; nor is it even the separation of a reality principle from a pleasure principle. It is an inaugural moment of a binary opposition which helps to *produce* the modern Western historical category of intellectual *work*, of serious knowledge. It is not just that children are socialized into accepting the difference between work and play; it is in the daily reproduction of the playground/classroom division that the category of serious knowledge is actually itself produced as a social practice, an institutional norm, and as a ruling idea. An enormous amount of teaching energy is expended in keeping the playground out of the classroom. With newer liberal teaching methods the classroom is sometimes taken out into the playground: educational games and toys colonize and 'clean up' playground culture and appropriate it for the purposes of education. But this is an entirely different thing from the radical interrogation of the 'lower' threshold of knowledge by the carnivalesque practices and rituals of the children themselves. 'Official' knowledge, encoded in high language constitutes itself over against low language and unofficial knowledge by excluding the latter from its own sovereign realm (or rather, by including it as excluded).

The playground/classroom split is only one institutionalizing moment of a process which will be continued, in a variety of ways and on a variety of fronts, all the way up the academic system into doctoral research and beyond. The 'serious business' of knowledge production will concern itself to no small degree simply with keeping itself 'serious', just as a teacher in the classroom spends much of the time ensuring that the space of knowledge—whatever that may be—is kept uncontaminated by low discourses. The 'seriousness' of the high language is in this respect anything but a neutral aspect of the material taught, it is not an intrinsic epistemological requirement. It is a power-category which endows the high language with the authority to exclude or to stigmatize low languages as disruptive, partisan, 'funny', one-sided, 'not-to-be-taken-seriously'.

The social reproduction of seriousness is a fundamental—perhaps *the* fundamental—hegemonic manœuvre. Once the high language has attained the commanding position of being able to specify what is and is not to be taken *seriously*, its control over the language of its society is virtually assured. Bakhtin calls this manœuvre 'the lie of pathos', which designates the insidious identification of 'important matters' with an idealism centred upon tragedy. There is an ambiguity at the heart of seriousness which all high language takes advantage of: the serious is at once that which excludes pleasurable laughter and that which is felt to be important. In fact of course there is no intrinsic link at all between these two things. Many solemn occasions and activities are utterly trivial, just as many 'laughable' incidents are important. Seriousness as the exclusion of laughter has much more to do with rituals of power and control than with thoughts intrinsically or essentially important. The compounding of the two is a ruse of reason, or, rather, a ruse of hegemonic language exorcizing threats to its authority. The 'lie of pathos' marks out the false solemnity of all 'official' languages which oppress people in and through their very seriousness.

7 Bakhtin, Sociolinguistics, and Deconstruction

In this essay I want to show that Bakhtin produced a theory of literature which encompassed and pushed beyond the present opposition between structural and sociolinguistic views of literary language. Moreover, since literary structuralism and deconstruction are ultimately linked to the same debate, I believe Bakhtin's theory simultaneously encompassed and pushed beyond them too. By 'pushed beyond', I mean that Bakhtin's work prefigured both structuralist and deconstructionist views of the language of literature, but crucially placed them both in a sociolinguistic framework which thereby makes them responsive to an historical and thoroughly social comprehension of literature. In other words, Bakhtin's theory of language can *give an account* of the split between structural and functional linguistics which is something neither tendency can do within its own terms.

For Bakhtin, language is conceived neither as a closed system of self-identical norms nor as a subjectively expressive medium, but as the concrete and ceaseless flow of *utterance* produced in dialogues between speakers in specific social and historical contexts. Throughout all his writing it is this emphasis on the centrality of dialogue, the dialectics of utterance, which grounds his ideas. His linguistic project set out to avoid abstract objectivism and individualistic subjectivism by centring its attention upon dialogic interaction.

Dialogue foregrounds speech diversity. Decades before they became of importance in sociolinguistics the concepts of sociolect and register were used by Bakhtin to explore the

First published in *The Theory of Reading*, ed. Frank Gloversmith (Brighton, 1984). All references in brackets are to Mikhail Bakhtin, *The Dialogic Imagination*, ed. M. Holquist, trans. C. Emerson and M. Holquist (Austin, Tex., 1981).

heteroglossia of social formations made manifest in discourse. Bakhtin writes:

At any given moment of its historical existence language is heteroglot from top to bottom: it represents the co-existence of socio-ideological contradictions between the present and the past, between different epochs of the past, between different socio-ideological groups in the present, between tendencies, schools, circles and so forth all given in bodily form. (p. 291)

Heteroglossia is Bakhtin's key term for describing the complex stratification of language into genre, register, sociolect, dialect, and the mutual interanimation of these forms. In 'Discourse in the Novel' he gives his most extended and detailed outline of the various elements which make up heteroglossia; it is clear that it covers a wide range of linguistic forms. Language is stratified according to social activity. Bakhtin does not use the term register, which was unavailable to him, but says:

There is interwoven with . . . generic stratification of language a *professional* stratification of language, in the broad sense of the term 'professional', the language of the lawyer, the doctor, the businessman, the politician, the public education teacher and so forth, and these sometimes coincide with, and sometimes depart from, the stratification into genres. (p. 289)

Bakhtin considers the formal linguistic markers of register indissociable from the intentional dimension of its meaning. To study only the formal linguistic features of different registers without understanding how they appropriate, possess, and dispossess language of specific concrete meanings is to produce a mere catalogue of dead forms. Every register is typification, a style, the bearer of specific socio-cultural intentions; at the same same time register is the bearer of self-referential identity which we recognize as such. Registers cannot help advertising themselves. We recognize them as pertaining to certain groups and certain social activities, hence as the registration of historical and social distinctions—not least power relations and hierarchies. Registers are thus not only a form of stratification, they are simultaneously language-images of stratification.

Furthermore, each social group or class stands in a different relation to the abstract system of the speech community in which it finds itself. Sociolects refer to the differential possession and concretizing of that system by different social groups defined by age, gender, economic position, kinship, relation, and so forth. Bakhtin has a much more conflict-centred view of sociolect than most linguists. Not only does he emphasize the way differences between the forms used to convey meaning identify and differentiate social groups, he sees sociolects as constantly struggling to attract words and linguistic forms into their own orbit, in order to reinflect them for their own use. Words are inflected by a certain sociolect so as to impose upon them 'specific semantic nuances and specific axiological overtones, thus [the sociolect] can create slogan-words, curse-words, praise-words and so forth' (p. 290). M. A. K. Halliday and Roger Fowler (the latter explicitly drawing on Bakhtin) have developed sociolinguistic analyses of groups in an antagonistic relation to the dominant culture: deviant subcultures, thieves, junkies, sexual 'perverts', convicts, political terrorists, street vandals, groups which systematically invert, negate, and relexicalize the norm language. It is this area of linguistic combat, the ideological interanimation between unmerged voices, which focuses dialogism. For Bakhtin, heteroglossia is not simply a range of sociolinguistic variation nor a kind of horizontal spread of dispersed speech forms: because languages are socially unequal, heteroglossia implies dialogic interaction in which the prestige languages try to extend their control and subordinated languages try to avoid, negotiate, or subvert that control. 'Language is not a neutral medium that passes freely and easily into the private property of the speaker's intentions: . . . Expropriating it, forcing it to submit to one's own intentions and accents, is a difficult and complicated process' (p. 294).

'The word in language is half someone else's' (p. 293). Language, intention, and ideology are inextricable for Bakhtin, and correspondingly, his concept of intention is a thoroughly linguistic one which involves a *directedness* towards objects and addressees, but always in a linguistic environment saturated with, and overlaid by, the intentions of others:

> But no living word relates to its object in a *singular* way: between the word and its object, between the word and the speaking subject, there exists an elastic environment of other alien words about the same object, the same theme, and this is an environment that is often difficult to penetrate. It is precisely in the process of living interaction with this specific environment that the word may be individualized and given stylistic shape. (p. 276)

This agonistic conception of the word struggling to achieve its intention amidst a throng of alien words is recalled in the work of Harold Bloom. Indeed, the *Anxiety of Influence* can be seen from this perspective as a precious and somewhat neuraesthenic version of the same idea. Bloom's 'strong poems' are those which succeed in the agonistic struggle against the alien word. How close Bloom is to Bakhtin when the latter writes:

> The word, breaking through to its own meaning and its own expression across an environment full of alien words and variously evaluating accents, harmonizing with some of the elements in this environment and striking a dissonance with others, is able, in this dialogizing process, to shape its own stylistic profile and tone. (p. 277)

Bakhtin and Bloom share a sense of the resistance put up by language against intention, as well as a sharp awareness of the consequent pattern within 'thousands of living dialogic threads' woven by consciousness around a given object. But whereas Bloom's heroes are romantic individualists, enlivened and ennervated by the pathos of solitary poetic combat, haunted by the need for strength (there is something enigmatically boyish about this desire for 'strongness' in Bloom), Bakhtin on the other hand generalizes the phenomenon into a broad sociological conception of language. *All* discourse, for Bakhtin, 'lives on the boundary between its own context and another, alien context (p. 284). Each and every time it is uttered, a word is recontextualized, pulled in a slightly different direction, imbued with a different inflection:

The word, directed towards its object, enters a dialogically agitated and tension-filled environment of alien words, value judgements and accents, weaves in and out of complex inter-relationships, merges with some, recoils from others, intersects with a third group: all this may crucially shape discourse, may complicate its expression and influence its entire stylistic profile. (p. 276)

What is striking about this passage is not so much its anticipation of a Derridean void inside discourse, carried here in Bakhtin's use of 'alien words', 'trace', and 'recoil', but its remarkable sense of heterogeneity as the living condition of language. Bakhtin uses a variety of rather vague metaphorical terms to grasp this quality of difference which words take on—a 'taste', 'profile', 'accent', 'inflection'—all suggesting something subtle and intimate in the difference made to the word in new contexts. This kind of meaning-variation is not normally addressed by formal semantics or socio-linguistics; it is somewhat literary in feeling. This is because, for Bakhtin, even individual words have 'style'. Like Vossler, Bakhtin believes in the precedence of style over grammar; that verbal forms generated in social interaction can later solidify into accepted grammatical norms. His linguistics therefore follows Vossler in this one respect that his studies on language stand on the boundary between stylistics and linguistics. He has a keen ear for what he terms the 'timbre' and the 'overtones' of words, and his insistence upon the 'multi-accentuality' of signs leads naturally to an interest in *the way words present themselves as representing*, their style of presence and address. Bakhtin richly develops the idea of dialogic interaction between 'high' and 'low' forms of language and it is this which prevents the concept of heteroglossia from degenerating into a mixed bag of socio-linguistic variables. Although separate aspects of heteroglossia (genre, register, sociolect, dialect, intertextuality, addressee-anticipation) can all be found under different names in current socio-linguistics, Bakhtin mobilizes them within a social dialectics of contention and negotiation. Heteroglossia not only foregrounds the words of people normally excluded from the realms of the 'norm' and the 'standard', it also relativizes the norm itself, subverting its claim to universalism. I think Bakhtin pushes the implications of this to such a point that it becomes a radical critique, not only of high language, but of any theory which tries to generalize and universalize on the basis of that high language, like say, transformational grammar. It is this reason that leads me to suggest that an understanding of heteroglossia may lead one to avoid not only the extravagance of most popular forms of deconstruction but also the restrictions of traditional structuralism.

Let me recall that in 1967 Uriel Weinreich, one of the founders of modern socio-linguistics and the teacher and mentor of William Labov, wrote: 'The facts of heterogeneity have not so far jibed well with the structural approach to language. . . . The solution . . . lies in the direction of breaking down the identification of structuredness with homogeneity.'[1] It is precisely this project—breaking down the identification of structuredness with homogeneity—which plays such an important part in Bakhtin. In his work heterogeneity is positive, productive, and enriching. He witnesses the perpetual unfolding of social heteroglossia surrounding objects, 'the Tower-of-Babel mixing of languages that goes on around any object; the dialectics of the object are interwoven with the social dialogue surrounding it' (p. 278). Not only is the word born in a dialogue with the alien words that already inhere in the object, it is born expecting an *answer*; 'every word is directed towards an answer and cannot escape the profound influence of the answering word that it anticipates' (p. 280). This is a new form of internal dialogism determined by its orientation towards the addressee. It is worth quoting Bakhtin at length:

The listener and his response are regularly taken into account when it comes to everyday dialogue and rhetoric, but every other sort of discourse as well is oriented towards an understanding that is 'responsive' although this orientation is not particularized in an independent act and is not compositionally marked . . . now this

---

[1] U. Weinreich, W. Labov, and M. Herzog, 'Empirical Foundations for a Theory of Language Change', in W. P. Lehmann and Y. Malkiel (eds.), *Directions for Historical Linguistics* (Austin, Tex., 1968), 100.

contradictory environment of alien words is present to the speaker not in the object, but rather in the consciousness of the listener, as his apperceptive background, pregnant with responses and objections. . . . Therefore his orientation towards the listener is an orientation toward a specific conceptual horizon, toward the specific world of the listener; it introduces totally new elements into his discourse; it is in this way, after all, that various different points of view, conceptual horizons, systems for providing expressive accents, various social 'languages' come to interact with one another. The speaker strives to get a reading on his own word . . . (pp. 280–2)

This line of dialogism is rhetorical. It is the distinctive form imparted to an utterance when it shapes itself to penetrate as deeply as possible the imagined resistance of its addressee. A kind of reader-oriented self-consciousness, it can be compared to the effect created in discourse by the 'implicit reader' spoken of by Wolfgang Iser. Every utterance is for or to someone, even if s/he is not actually present, and the dialogic anticipation of response is always already inscribed in language as it is spoken. This does not necessarily imply subterfuge. It means, however, that words will be inflected in a slightly new or different way, nuanced to gain power for themselves. As the addressee changes, so do they. Again this is by no means a purely subjective matter: the word is projected toward an alien conceptual horizon which is ideologically illuminated. Bakhtin thus anticipated much of the current German thinking about reception and there are various points at which reception theory and dialogism may be connected up; however, that cannot be covered here. What I wish to emphasize is that dialogism is oriented in two directions at once, towards the object (theme) and towards the addressee, both exerting active pressure on the profile and formation of the word.

Let me recall Ulrich Weinreich's exhortation to break down the habitual identification of structuredness with homogeneity. Bakhtin has a strong sense of structure—indeed we should expect as much from a thinker whose work was so closely intertwined with that of the Formalists in the 1920s. In 'Forms of Time and of the Chronotope in the

Novel', he explores a wide range of scene and narrative structures in fiction from the Ancient Greeks to Flaubert. But he always considered plot in the novel to be the articulation of different language-images or verbal-ideological discourses. 'In a word', he says, 'the novelistic plot serves to represent speaking persons and their ideological worlds' (p. 365).

But unlike the early Propp, or many modern structuralists, Bakhtin never envisages structure as transcendental. The authority of structure (political, narrative, and syntactic) is socially constructed and historically changing. It is only in societies isolated from significant linguistic diversity that structures of narrative (underpinned by a unified, homogeneous, and therefore 'absolute' language) appear to have complete authority—the authority, precisely, of *myth*. For Bakhtin, there is a decisive moment in the life of a speech community when it encounters powerful language other than its own. Suddenly, everything changes under the pressure of this new-found 'polyglossia', 'the simultaneous presence of two or more national languages interacting within a single cultural system' (p. 431 n.). This moment of polyglossia relativizes the 'host' language and displaces it, opening out a distance between language and reality in such a way as to bring both into view for the first time.

After all, it is possible to objectivize one's own particular language, its internal form, the peculiarities of its world view, its specific linguistic habitus, only in the light of another language belonging to someone else, which is almost as much 'one's own' as one's 'native language' . . . where languages and cultures interanimate each other, language became something entirely different, its very nature changes: in place of a single, unitary sealed-off Ptolemaic world of language, there appeared the open Galilean world of many languages, mutually animating each other. (pp. 62–5)

This movement, in a given speech community, from monoglossia to polyglossia is of extraordinary significance. Two myths perish simultaneously: 'the myth of a language that presumes to be the only language, and the myth of a language that presumes to be completely unified' (p. 68). Certain traditional genres such as myth, epic, and tragedy are the products of a centralizing tendency in language, a monoglossic absolutism. This is why structuralism works so well for these genres: sealed off from heteroglossia, they are immune from an intertextual interference. Nothing can intervene across their endless cycles of telling and retelling, production and consumption, to alter the strong regularities which have solidified into their sequence of articulation. They are the narrative equivalent of what Marx called 'simple reproduction' in the economic sphere. That is, a kind of discursive economy which cannot expand its base because it has not developed a division of (linguistic) labour to any significant extent. This static cycle of simple reproduction leads to the constant repetition of a pattern of self-identical norms, which of course is precisely what a system or structure consists of. Structuralism tends to look towards monoglossia to provision its best research. By contrast, polyglossia begins to free consciousness from the tyranny of its own language and its own myth of language. Languages gradually become visible as different, they emerge as 'language-images' which can be represented, set over against one another, tested and contested. The novel, for Bakhtin, is a more extensive genre than normally conceived and is born from this interanimation of language-images. His most cogent definition of the novel describes it as 'a diversity of social speech types (sometimes even a diversity of languages) and a diversity of individual voices, artistically organized' (p. 262). The Roman Empire and the Renaissance were both, according to Bakhtin, periods of marked polyglossia, and in both periods novelistic genres emerged as a result. Menippean Satire, Ovid's *Metamorphosis*, Apuleius's *Golden Ass*, are the novelistic fictions which emerge from ancient Rome, a culture which, Bakhtin says:

at the outset was characterized by tri-lingualism—Greek, Oscan and Roman. Lower Italy was the home of a specific kind of hybrid culture and hybrid literary forms. The rise of Roman literature is connected in a fundamental way with this trilingual cultural home; this literature was born in the interanimation of three languages—one that was indigenously its own, and two that were other but that were experienced as indigenous. (p. 63)

'Oscan' is important to Bakhtin's argument about both Roman and Renaissance literature. It was from the Oscans that the Romans derived a kind of crude farce called Atellanae, which *The Dictionary of Greek and Roman Geography* defines as resembling

the performances of Pulcinello, still so popular at Naples and its neighbourhood. When they were transplanted to Rome they were naturally rendered into Latin; but though Strabo is probably mistaken in speaking of the Fabulae Atellanae of his day as still performed at Rome in Oscan, it is very natural to suppose that they were still so exhibited in Campania so long as the Oscan language continued in common use in that country.[2]

The Atellanae provide fascinating evidence for Bakhtin's persistent linking of carnival farce, novelistic form, and polyglossia, and it is food for thought that the Atellanae, instrumental in the dialogizing of the literature of ancient Rome, may also have been instrumental (in the transformed guise of Neapolitan folk comedy) in dialogizing Renaissance literature in the way that Bakhtin suggests in *Rabelais and his World*.

Trained in classical philology, Bakhtin is acutely attentive to this hybridization—the influencing and mixing of distinct language-strains. In the Renaissance he sees the birth of modern narratives like *Don Quixote*, *Gargantua*, and *Pantagruel* as crucially determined by an active polyglossia, a dialogic interaction between 'high' classical languages (chivalric romance, sermon, homily, idealist philosophies) and 'low' vernaculars (anecdotes, street-strongs, folk-sayings, the languages of the street, the square, the market-place, and the carnival). It is this dialogic relation between high and low languages which became the foundation of his brilliant study of *Rabelais and his World*, in which he shows carnival languages of the common people 'playing up' against the tragic pathos and high seriousness of the dominant artistic, moral, and political discourses of the period. In this view the 'earthy' folk word—scatalogical, irreverent, humorous, and

---

[2] *The Dictionary of Greek and Roman Geography*, ed. W. Smith (London, 1856), i. 253.

contradictory—becomes both a critique of, and corrective to, the lie of pathos. The lofty word of authority is 'brought down a peg or two'. In polyglossia the focus of interest for Bakhtin is not merely the interanimation of 'equal' languages, but the interanimation of high with low, the conflicts engendered when the dominant, centralizing, and unifying language of a hegemonic group is contested by the low language of subordinated classes.

In the modern novel Bakhtin's notion of polyglossia is of decisive importance. Julia Kristeva, together with writers of the once radical *Tel Quel* group in France, have emphasized the polyphonic qualities of major modernist factions. The hybridization of voices in *Ulysses* and *Finnegans Wake*, the parodying and deflation of the language of authority by low languages, is a fundamental feature of Joyce's work. The Catholic Mass, the Lord's Prayer, the high languages of aesthetics, philosophy, and politics, find themselves pulverized by 'common' forms of language—the language of the pub, the gutter press, the brothel, of Dublin working-class life, the market-place, and the bedroom. Blocks and fragments of language interanimate one another, recontextualizing familiar class, gender, and racial styles so that each is reinflected, made strange, or even made questionable by the mobility of context. Official and authoritative languages are plagued by parodic echoes and jokey versions of their sacred words. Even the counterpoint of Stephen Dedalus and Leopold Bloom can be seen, not only as a Don Quixote–Sancho Panza double act, but as a dialogic play of high against low. Stephen's priggish intellectualism collides with Bloom's ingenuous obsession with body and bowels; again and again throughout the day, spiritual intensity is discomfited by the material world of the 'bodily lower strata' of buttocks, belly, and feet.

Both *Ulysses* and *Finnegans Wake* are thoroughly carnivalesque in Bakhtin's sense. The opening lines of *Ulysses*, in which 'Stately, plump Buck Mulligan' travesties the Mass, inaugurates a dialogic interplay which will be amplified throughout the text into a total polyphony:

He held the bowl aloft and intoned:
—*Introibo ad altare Dei.*
Halted, he peered down the dark winding stairs and called up coarsely:
—Come up, Kinch. Come up, you fearful jesuit.[3]

In discussing medieval literature Bakhtin underlines the central role of 'degradation' through comic parody or semi-parody of Church Latin forms. 'Cyprian's supper' (*coena Cypriani*) was a peculiar festive travesty of the entire Scriptures; in *Rabelais and his World* Bakhtin remarks that 'the influence of the carnival spirit was irresistible: it made a man renounce his official state as monk, cleric, scholar, and perceive the world in its laughing aspect . . . *Monkish pranks* (*Joca monacorum*) was the title of one of the most popular medieval comic pieces.'[4]

It is striking that one of the great works of modern literature should open with hybrid linguistic form, a monkish prank on the part of the irreverent iconoclast Mulligan at the expense of the 'fearful jesuit' Dedalus which, by parodying the Latin Mass, replays Renaissance student combat between high language (Latin, the Church) and the Vulgate.

It is not my purpose here to apply Bakhtin's ideas in any sustained way to particular novels. A full Bakhtinian analysis of *Ulysses* would be an extraordinarily fruitful enterprise. It is worth nothing, however, that Joyce is almost alone in earlier modern fiction in rejecting the 'lie of tragic pathos' through polyglossia and thus, whilst *he* can be seen as a true inheritor of the carnivalesque spirit, there are many modern writers who recuperate the use of polyglossia so as to reinforce the authority of high languages. Often this is done through a kind of 'stalemating' of sociolects and registers, whereby the cacophony of voices indicates not a robust debunking of powerful groups but a chaos of competing voices, a dissonant chorus wailing within some twentieth-century necropolis.

[3] J. Joyce, *Ulysses* (Harmondsworth, 1969), 9.
[4] M. Bakhtin, *Rabelais and his World*, trans. H. Iswolsky (Cambridge, Mass., 1968), 13 and 85.

Malcolm Lowry's *Under the Volcano* appears to be a work of the modern carnivalesque. Not only does its story take place on the day of a great fiesta, a real Mexican carnival, the elements of which are woven into the content of the hero's life, but it is self-consciously polyphonic. English, Spanish, Aztec, French, and German make up its active polyglossia, whilst the inebriate, bar-room dialogues of its increasingly drunken protagonist are played off against the authority of traditional literature (Faust, Shakespeare, Romanticism, Conrad) and of dominant discourses (diplomacy, geography, national history). But the fiesta is the Day of the Dead and the polyphony is that of Babel. The consul 'proudly insists' that the ruined pyramid which dominates Cholula is 'the original Tower of Babel' and the novel spirals into a confusion of tongues, a tragic chaos portending the consul's incomprehension and death:

'My tongue is dry in my mouth for the want of *our* speech. If you let anything happen to yourself you will be harming my flesh and mind. I am in your hands now. Save—'

'Mexican works, England works, Mexican works, sure, French works. Why speak English? Mine Mexican, Mexican United States he sees *Negros*—de comprende—Detroit, Houston, Dallas . . .'

'¿Quiere usted la salvación de Méjico? ¿Quiere usted que Cristo sea nuestro Rey?'

'No.'[5]

Here is an exemplary polyglossia, not only mobilizing Yvonne's pleading—'My tongue is dry in my mouth for the want of *our* speech'—words written in a letter—in such a way as to equate lost love with the alienation of speech; but also invoking the cacophony of the bar (its Spanish radio programme, the consul's drunken ramblings, and the conversation of the Mexican) as a metonymy of breakdown—the consul's and also the world's, for each is slithering to its own ravine, the consul to his grave and the world to the Second World War (it is 1938). Here then, polyglossia is pressed

---

[5] M. Lowry, *Under the Volcano* (Harmondsworth, 1976), 367.

back into the service of romantic pathos, recuperated through its evocation of alienated misunderstanding and irreducible foreignness. 'Our speech' has become lost in the clamour of heteroglossia, a sea of tragic babble. *Under the Volcano* rejects any form of salvation and the consul's monosyllabic 'No' to the rhetorical enquiry of the radio as to the desire for salvation (of Mexico, of the soul) underwrites the form of the book as a whole. Often highly comic in its parody of high language (I particularly remember the consul's drunken misreadings of Dr Vigil's visiting-card, turning his list of certificates, diplomas, and university qualifications into a bizarre enumeration of sexual debility), the novel nevertheless operates overall to stay within a religious and Faustian myth of a fall without resurrection. Its complex heteroglossia (to which I can do no more than gesture here) does not automatically produce a carnivalesque subversion of the old hierarchies.

A more complex case than either *Ulysses* or *Under the Volcano* is provided by the novels of Thomas Pynchon. Again, *The Crying of Lot 49*, *V*, and *Gravity's Rainbow* appear to provide perfect examples of Bakhtin's thesis. The high languages of modern America—technology, psychoanalysis, business, administration, and military jargon—are 'carnivalized' by a set of rampant, irreverent, inebriate discourses from low life—from the locker-room, the sewers (in *V*), the jazz club and cabaret, New York Yiddish, student fraternities, and GI slang. In *Gravity's Rainbow* history is referred to as a 'St Giles's Fair', and the symbolic pig, the carnival animal *par excellence*, wallows everywhere in Pynchon's writing as the foul-mouthed but irrepressible subvert of prissy WASP orderliness. Krinkles Porcino, 'Pig' Bodine, Porky Pig, and others grunt their indulgent, sardonic disapproval of American corporate Enterprise. Dozens of different registers, dialects, sociolects, and even national languages interanimate each other in Pynchon's work to provide a dazzling intertextuality of misquotation and bizarre dialogue. But Pynchon does not simply amalgamate or relativize a host of different language-forms. He produces a dialogic confrontation whereby power and authority are probed and ritually contested by these debunking vernaculars.

The result, however, is different both from the positive carnival of *Ulysses* and the romantic dissolution of *Under the Volcano*. Pynchon neutralizes the conflict of high and low language by framing it within narratives of enigma. He appears, again and again in his stories, to reject *both* the high and the low, setting them off against each other in hilarious scenes which unnervingly flip over into sinister intimations of death and apocalypse. *Gravity's Rainbow* is strangely like a *Ulysses* written by Lowry mixed into *Under the Volcano* written by Joyce: a feast of words is set against conspiracies of holocaust and war. At any second in the Byzantine plot a wisecrack may became a clue to violent political apocalypse, or the hieratic language of ALGOL become comic-book farce. Pynchon's heteroglossia occupies an ambiguous middle ground between those of the other two writers. His fascinated disgust at the carnivalesque decadence of his low discourses (the language of the Whole Sick Crew) is matched by his conspiracy view of the international corporate systems of capitalism. The heteroglossia becomes immobilized into a cold war without positive issue, absurd and terrifying at once.

Bakhtin is perfectly aware that the polar opposition between a sealed-off and impermeable monoglossia and a developing polyglossia is something of a fiction. Elsewhere he writes: 'It is our conviction that there never was a single strictly straightforward genre, no single type of direct discourse—artistic, rhetorical, philosophical, religious, ordinary everyday—that did not have its own parodying and travestying double, its own comic-ironic *contre-partie*' (p. 53).

What they represent, however, are two fundamental tendencies: monoglossia embodies the hegemonic force of a language established as 'the' language of the speech community, unified, centralized, authoritative, always *mythic* because unrelativized and unpunctured by travesty. Polyglossia embodies the forces of dispersal and differentiation, the reality of actual speech situations, their disjunctions and productive heterogeneity. The movement of a speech community from monoglossia to polyglossia may best be thought of as similar to the movement of a social formation from *simple reproduction* to *expanded reproduction*. This is not, of course, to posit any perfect 'fit' or homology à la Goldmann between economic structure and linguistic development. But there is an obvious correlation between an increasing division of labour and a growth of new linguistic registers, the latter providing precisely a heteroglot potentiality for the development of intertextuality (and hence of 'novel' forms). Monoglossia and polyglossia are thus *tendencies* rather than strictly separable stages in the life of a speech community. Thus, even after a society has engaged with another language as a deeply important part of its own culture, monoglossia tends to reassert itself, one language attempts to gain hegemony, to incorporate the new.

Just as structuralism has an affinity for genres which pertain to monoglossia, deconstruction can be seen as an attempt to grasp the conflicting heterogeneities of language, rewriting its heteroglot difference as precisely the impossibility of a master discourse, the impossibility of an invulnerable metalanguage.

This may seem an eccentric way to come at deconstruction, but when we realize that a fundamental form of dialogism exists between speaking and writing, then the project of a *grammatology* is revealed for what it is, a simple metaphysical inversion of the old hierarchy which gave ontological priority to speech over writing. In fact, the relation of written forms to spoken forms in any speech community is a historical question, one which Derrida fails to address because he has a purely *metaphysical* notion of heteroglossia insulated from the transformative and conflictual social arena of speech events.

As far as I understand it, deconstruction is an attack upon traditional tenets of Western philosophy carried out through a close critical unpicking of the language of some 'key' texts. Deconstruction shows that language does not simply 'come after' the concepts it is supposed to represent, like some kind of delayed supplement or exposition. For Derrida, language ensnares and defeats rationality, rendering some of its fundamental categories—origin, presence, meaning—perfectly useless. Derrida does this in three ways. Firstly, he pushes to breaking-point Saussure's idea that a language is only constituted by differences without positive terms. Meaning resides in the pertinent distinctions made *between* signifiers in a system, not in the individual terms of the system. Thus, the meaning of any term employed in discourse is determined by its difference from a set of elements *not present* in that discourse. Its pre-condition for meaning, then, is always absent, always elsewhere, like a horizon we can never reach. The moment of full meaning, the plenitude of presence, when the end of the chain of signification will be reached, never comes: full presence is endlessly deferred, it is always 'in *différance*'. Secondly, rational finality will always be frustrated because concepts never escape from metaphor, and syntax never escapes from rhetoric. However hard the thinker tries to produce a self-sustaining 'pure' reason, the thinking is always 'engrained' in metaphor and 'bedevilled' by rhetoric. Thirdly, however much we think we are thinking only with ideas, the actual phonetic and graphic material of language is constantly drifting our thought along currents of its own. The words we choose to express ourselves are influenced by the sounds or the shapes of the signifiers already produced. Everyone is familiar with that irritating habit words have of settling on the end of the pen so that they return again and again over a few pages. Likewise rhymes, rhythms, cadences, homonyms, assonance, and alliteration all have their subtly determining effect upon what and how we write. What Mallarmé called 'la musique dans les lettres' is a prose as well as poetic phenomenon. The patterning and flux of phonic and graphic material cannot be discounted as a determiner of meaning in discourse.

These three points (albeit briefly and crudely sketched) seem not implausible. What is implausible is the exaggerated claim made for them by deconstruction. Reading deconstructive criticism in both its French and American varieties one comes to believe that all discursive paths are dead ends or labyrinths which turn back upon themselves. Indeed the rhetorical figure for this is 'doubt', *aporia* (from the Greek meaning 'unpassable road'), and *aporia* has become the transcendental signified of deconstruction. With a mixture of playful mischief and pathos, the would-be Derrideans find that all traces of meaning lead to paradox, absence, and doubt, which for them become the signifiers of the text. Deconstruction is a carnival of scepticism, demythologizing the pretentious claims of monoglossia, demystifying the complete, sovereign, philosophic word, yet hermetically sealed in a Saussurean problematic which fails to understand the positive, socially constitutive role of heteroglossia. It is true of course that in a famous essay founding grammatology, Derrida rigorously criticized Saussure. But the focus of his critique was the way Saussure subordinated 'writing' (in the large, Derridean sense) to speaking. Bakhtin's critique of Saussure (one of the linguists who produced an 'abstract objectivism') is more radical and far-reaching than Derrida's, despite the Nietzschean panache of the latter. For Bakhtin, language is also split, conflict-ridden, dispersed, and drastically heterogeneous. But as well it is systematic, highly coded, patterned, and regular. Both poles, the homogeneous and heterogeneous, operate to produce meaning, and from this dialectical perspective Bakhtin can analyse a whole range of speech events in their historical specificity, according to their social group, context, and power relations. Only for those who identify language as such with Saussurean *langue* does it appear paradoxical and impossible that dispersal, *différance*, lacks, absence, traces, and all the other modes of radical heterogeneity should be there at the heart of discourses which pretend to be complete. Much of the time, deconstruction is rediscovering in texts, with a kind of bemused fascination, all the indices of heteroglossia which Saussure had excluded from consideration in his own model, by consigning them to the trash-can of 'parole'. To discover that rationality (the logic of the signified) may be subverted by writing itself (the logic of the signifier) seems to put the 'whole of the Western episteme' into jeopardy, but is in fact a fairly trivial business. This triviality is one of the reasons why deconstruction has so quickly found that its natural *métier* is fairground nonsense and game-playing. When Derrida deliberately played the fool at Searle's expense in the *Glyph* exchange, ridiculing his name, punning, cracking jokes, changing masks like a comedian, he was doing nothing more than we should expect, he was fulfilling the natural role of deconstruction as a carnivalization monoglossia. The *Glyph* essays of Derrida put me in mind of this passage from Bakhtin:

> At the time when poetry (and we may add, philosophy) was accomplishing the task of cultural, national and political centralization of the verbal-ideological world in the higher official socio-ideological levels, on the lower levels, on the stages of local fairs and at buffoon spectacles, the heteroglossia of the clown sounded forth, ridiculing all 'languages' and dialects; there developed the literature . . . where there was no language centre at all, where there was to be found a lively play with the 'languages' of poets, scholars, monks, knights and others, where all languages were masks and where no language could claim to be an authentic and incontestable face. (pp. 272–3)

This, surely, is the deconstructionist project. Insisting upon a 'language with no centre at all', ridiculing all languages and dialects, Derrida constantly makes 'lively play' with the 'languages' of poets and scholars (monks, knights, and others rather less often, I grant). Indeed, a key strategy of grammatology was to confound genres by cutting across the usual boundaries between poetry, literary criticism, philosophy, and fiction, mocking the seriousness and haughty autonomy of each—'the heteroglossia of the clown sounded forth'. Deconstruction is a compromised, idealist carnival so obsessed with rooting out metaphysical error that it remains enmeshed—if only by dependent negation—upon metaphysics itself. It sets out to carnivalize the pretentious academic word by destroying monoglossia from within—a project doomed because to remain within monoglossia is to retain a base in metaphysics rather than in social history. The luxury of 'endless deferral' is only available to those who play with themselves in the abstract idealist realm of *langue*. The real social difference of heteroglossia in fact puts a swift end to the unmotivated *différance* of Derridean discourse: Derridean *différance* evaporates once you move from *langue* to *parole*, or from competence to performance. The trick of deconstruction is to treat texts not as specific performances within a social discourse, but as abstract repertoires of competence. As soon as you do this, then all the terms of the repertoire become ambiguous and fall away from each other. They are no longer held together by the social motivations, functions, and uses of the discourse, but fall back into their plurality of potential. By contrast, the differences which Bakhtin registers in heteroglossia encode real social differences. For him inequality of power and access are already inscribed in the way language shifts to resist, negotiate, or accommodate a realm saturated with alien words, other people's words.

Bakhtin recognized that any abstract objectivist theory of language always went hand in hand with the language of the dominant social class. High languages are imperialistic. They establish themselves as both 'standard' and prestige by a variety of methods, including 'objective' grammars, the prescription of norms, structural theories of language (and even deconstructive theories), in so far as all these systematically exclude the actual speech use of the majority of people. All theories of *langue*, deep structure, basic systemic sentences, and *différance* are metaphysical in that they are attempts to isolate a pure and unmotivated language anterior to the use of actual speech by social groups. But this abstract *langue* is nothing other than the modern myth of a perfect monoglossia, universal and unitary only in the abstract. The principal social function served by these theories of language is to act as sophisticated agents of cultural unification and centralization. *Langue*, and all theories derived from it, are but the homogenizing power of myth over language, or of metaphysics over utterance. The only place where *langue* and its deconstruction actually exist is in the (highly motivated) *utterances* of the professional linguist or philosopher, in the high languages of academic culture.

Bakhtin's work seems to me to transcend both deconstruction and structuralism by revealing each to be a one-sided abstraction from the lived complexity of language. On the one hand, structuralism, following Saussure, treats language as *langue* by isolating unified structures within monoglossia. This works well for monoglossic societies, as the work of Vernant, Vidal-Nacquet, and Detienne on Greek tragedy and myth has shown. Like Propp's work on folk-tale, and that of Alan Dundes and Lévi-Strauss on myth, structuralism (for reasons elaborated above) finds its 'good object' of study in monoglossia. But structuralism notoriously failed to produce a significant and convincing theory of the novel, since it is, through and through, a heteroglot composition—a multi-accented, hybrid construction which requires both structuralist *and* socio-linguistic analysis. The novel *plays with the historical and social boundaries* of speech types, languages, and belief systems, and is thus irreducible to the norms governing any one of them. It is, as Bakhtin notes, a 'militantly protean' form, always novel when it appears, feeding on its own variation and self-criticism. This places it beyond the reach of any theory like structuralism which seeks *systematic* regularity as its exhaustive protocol.

On the other hand, deconstruction abstracts only those aspects of language where intention and unity appear to falter. It is like a geological map of language which marks out the slippage, the fault-lines, and the crevices, but omits all the strata and formations between them. Whereas Bakhtin sees both formations and their fractures as constitutive of style and meaning, the deconstructionist sees only the fault-lines; an impasse, a *non plus ultra*. Bakhtin's socio-linguistic knowledge gives him a more inclusive understanding of how discourse works than the deconstructionists, for whom—most of the time—discourse fails to work at all (it plays). Bakhtin writes:

It is precisely the diversity of speech, and not the unity of a normative shared language, that is the ground of a style. . . . Even in those places where the author's voice seems at first glance to be unitary and consistent, direct and immediately intentional, beneath that smooth single-languaged surface we can nevertheless uncover prose's three-dimensionality, its profound speech diversity, which enters the project of style and is its determining factor. (pp. 308, 315)

This has something in common with the deconstructive view, but it is informed by a broader sociological sense of discourse as a functioning ensemble, creating its identity (style) through an exploitation of language diversity. Thus, throughout Bakhtin's essays we encounter passages which seem impeccably 'structuralist' and elsewhere strikingly 'deconstructionist'. By centring his theoretical understanding of language upon dialogic utterance, he fuses the insights of both schools into a critical socio-linguistics of culture which supersedes both.

'Critical socio-linguistics of culture' was carefully chosen. I think it is clear how Bakhtin fulfils the dictum of Weinreich, already quoted, about breaking down the identification of structure with homogeneity. Bakhtin studied the historical mobility of discourses through the dynamic of language pulled in one direction by the structural unity of monoglossia, and in the other direction by heteroglot speech diversities of genre, register, dialect, sociolect, cohabitation, and intertextuality. What puts him beyond most current socio-linguistics (however unsystematic his attention to the full range of speech variation) is that his work is critical as well as descriptive. He is aware, even when writing about something as apparently remote as Renaissance comedy, that speech diversity in class society indexes actual inequality. This is not meant in a Bernstein sense and has nothing to do with the quarrel about restricted and elaborated codes: there is nothing in Bakhtin to suggest he thought one language any better or worse than another. But he emphasizes that the centralizing and unifying of language is a crucial act of hegemony by a powerful social group. 'Thus a unitary language gives expression to forces working towards concrete verbal and ideological unification and centralization, which develop in vital connection with the process of sociopolitical and cultural centralization' (p. 271).

The brilliant stroke in Bakhtin—and what saves his work from falling into crude 'reflectionism' whereby language simply mirrors class—is in his dynamic model of language in which centripetal forces seek to unify and homogenize it against centrifugal forces which seek to pull it apart. These opposed pressures or tendencies keep language mobile just as they are responsible for its transformations. What is more, any theory of unified language becomes itself a key agency in the struggle, and is itself one of the forces which serve to unify and centralize the verbal-ideological world. It is this informing sense of hegemonic struggle which makes Bakhtin a Kulturkritiker as well as a descriptive socio-linguist. The key passage is worth quoting at length:

Aristotelian poetics, the poetics of Augustine, the poetics of the medieval Church, of 'the one language of truth', the Cartesian poetics of neoclassicism, the abstract grammatical universalism of Leibniz (the idea of 'universal grammar'), Humboldt's insistence on the concrete—all these, whatever their differences in nuance, give expression to the same centripetal forces in sociolinguistic and ideological life; they serve one and the same project of centralizing and unifying the European languages. The victory of one reigning language (dialect) over the others, the supplanting of languages, their enslavement, the process of illuminating them with the True Word, the incorporation of barbarians and lower social strata into a unitary language of culture and truth, the canonization of ideological systems . . . all this determined the content and power of the category of 'unitary language' in linguistic and stylistic thought, and determined its creative, style-shaping role in the majority of the poetic genres that coalesced in the channel formed by those same centripetal forces of verbal-ideological life. (p. 271)

Bakhtin reveals the intimate connection between theories based upon a unified conception of language and the development towards hegemony of that language itself. There is an especially snug 'fit' between linguistic theories of abstract objectivism and a process of socio-political and cultural centralization. Grammar, poetics, and unitary language theory are modes whereby the prestige language simultaneously canonizes itself, regularizes and endorses its system and boundaries, makes itself teachable and assimilable in educational practice, and above all 'naturalizes' itself over against all competing sociolects, dialects, and registers.

Interestingly, Bakhtin's assertion is supported by Charles Ferguson's seminal 1959 article in *Word* in which he coined the term diglossia (a preliminary version of Ferguson's study had been entitled 'Classical or Colloquial, One Standard or Two'—a title with a certain Bakhtinian ring about it). This term, diglossia, describes the situation of those speech communities in which two or more varieties of the same language are used by the same speakers under different conditions. As examples, he took Swiss German, Arabic, Modern Greek, and Haitian Creole, all four speech communities which operate both with a 'superimposed prestige' form of the language ('high') and with regional dialects ('low'). Ferguson's description of this situation[6] perfectly confirms Bakhtin's own work. But Ferguson's work—and indeed much of the socio-linguistic research on diglossia since 1959—is content to register and describe the interrelation between prestige forms and low forms. Indeed, Deuchar and Martin-Jones (in a paper presented to the Sociolinguistics Symposium at Sheffield in March 1982) remark that 'It is not clear to what extent variation theory (the dominant approach of current sociolinguistics) constitutes a theory, since so much attention is devoted in this approach to the description of the facts of linguistic variation with relatively little reference to explanation.'[7] They also remark, acerbically and with perfect justification, that 'those who describe themselves as sociolinguists do not appear to have a social theory'.[8] Bakhtin, however, pursues the political and cultural point made in passing in the quotation given above (p. 126). The H-form becomes the prestige or standard in a variety of ways which are all linked to the socio-economic and political power of a given group or class. The specific H-form is con-

---

[6] See the beginning of Ch. 6, p. 126.

[7] M. Deuchar and M. Martin-Jones, 'Linguistic Research in Majority and Minority Communities: Goals and Methods', unpublished paper presented at the Sociolinguistics Symposium, Sheffield, Mar. 1982, 4.

[8] Ibid. 7.

stituted as unitary through the agencies of scholars, lexico-graphers, grammarians, and literary critics, thus becoming a centripetal force of language in a political process of central-ization and incorporation.

Much of Bakhtin's work can be read as a brilliant, lightly disguised polemic against the process of centralization and State domination going on in Russia during the period of Stalinism. By championing the heteroglossia of the 'folk' against the imposed authority of monoglossia, he was implic-itly criticizing from a populist perspective the 'dismal sacred word' of ruthless State centralization. But Bakhtin's penetrat-ing comprehension of hegemonic violence and popular forms of resistance to incorporation in the realm of discourse speaks directly to us, too. The question of heteroglossia, cor-rectly addressed, focuses analysis on the political realities informing all levels of cultural production, from the sophisti-cation of transformational grammar down to dirty jokes. Without ever diminishing the utopian ideals of play and plea-sure which deconstruction embodies, Bakhtin nevertheless shows up, through and through, the ludic narcissism at the heart of the deconstructionist project. Even more, he reveals the naïve complicity deconstruction may have with social control and domination, and the consequent role that dia-logic resistance must play to disrupt this.

8 Prosthetic Gods in Atrocious Places: Gilles Deleuze/Francis Bacon

Francis Bacon's art is a critique of the 'Beautiful and the True' in the name of a grotesque and other truth: phobic psychopathology of daily life. This phobic substratum is known intimately to the hysteric and marks out a degree zero of culture. Corporeal, convulsive, the great fear at the heart of every Bacon painting has no story to tell, nothing to narrate, and appears even more terrible than the exorbitant fears in Lautréamont, Kafka, Beckett, and Bataille, where a fleeting displacement on to the narrative axis of desire affords some small release. The hysterical fear of which Bacon's great paintings are the immediate registration is mutant, an unfixing of identity without end or issue. Bacon thereby portrays what Sartre merely posited: the *viscosity* of fear, or fear imaged as a melting, a falling, a queasiness of guts and flesh in which the body itself dissolves into liquid flow.

Bacon's great wager is that these hysterical representations speak not just out of his own psychopathology but to and of the present age. He displays the intellectual ruthlessness of a sublime cultural interrogator—the Grand Inquisitor of modern painting—and the subjects of his interrogation are the contemporary culture, his fellow artists, the great European painters of the tradition and himself. I believe Bacon when he says that his paintings are not about horror. He reveals himself in each canvas too relentlessly intelligent and too solitary to stage-manage a paint horror-show. The unspeakable phobic texture of the paintings is shocking, but Bacon goes to great lengths to avoid the inflated sensationalizing of horror which has become a

Review, previously unpublished, written 1983, of Gilles Deleuze, *Francis Bacon: Logique de la sensation*, 2 vols. (Paris, 1981). References in brackets are to volume, page, and plate-numbers in Deleuze.

staple of mass culture. Indeed Bacon's paintings are all the more disturbing for their fastidious dialogue with mass cultural stereotypes (*The Elephant Man* is an interesting exception in that Bacon's self-portraits bear a startling resemblance to Meyrick in the final acute phase of his illness, but this might well have to do with Bacon's acknowledged use of medical textbooks as a source of grotesque material). Curiously, I now think his paintings are, with one or two exceptions, deliberately understated. At first I only saw an atrocious subversion of the classical canon but I now see an awesome patience and thoughtfulness behind the self-hatred and transgressive violence. And in some measure Bacon has won his wager, pitting his intelligence and intransigence against hysteria and wrestling from it a significant critical representation of our culture.

The interior terror and subliminal anxiety which turn our bodies into the battleground of our fears also make the effort of controlled representation almost hopeless. Bacon's paintings, however, though obsessive, are never uncontrolled, even in their noted incorporation of accidental brush-strokes. And for me this considerable achievement, which blends hysteria and intellectual self-control, is matched by Bacon's radical refusal of transcendence—a firm refusal of narrative and a refusal of sublimation. There is a kind of material resolution in the paintings, which amounts to a modern heroism, not to allow conventional beauty to obliterate or falsify the moments of abjection which permeate daily life. The blasphemy of his triptychs and crucifixions is their immediate attachment to present flesh. One of the many dialogues, or contestations, which Bacon is involved in is with the transcendental escapism of the European painting tradition. First with the major forms of religious and classical iconography and secondly with the aesthetic formalism of his bourgeois contemporaries. If his paintings are claustrophobic it is partly because he has deliberately and almost systematically closed off the idealist exits conventionally held open. However painful to witness, the perverse integrity of Bacon's decision over forty years to privilege abjection rather than to sanctify the sublime has produced a singular achievement.

Gilles Deleuze's book *Francis Bacon: Logique de la sensation* provides an elegant, incisive reading of the formal qualities of Bacon's paintings. Once again, as with the books on Proust and Kafka, Deleuze demonstrates his skill at combining close and attentive reading of particular art forms with an iconoclastic disregard for psychological and sociological properties. In seventeen short essay-sections he focusses upon themes, aspects, and the formal qualities of Bacon's *œuvre* and produces brilliant readings of the paintings (which are supplied in a well-illustrated companion volume which displays the paintings in the order in which Deleuze discusses them). Starting with the circle or oval in which Bacon habitually encloses his figures, Deleuze catalogues and discusses the compositional, thematic, and technical procedures of Bacon's work with a panache which makes each of the seventeen sections an independent virtuoso performance. He discusses Bacon's use of sculptural modelling to give his figures an alarming deliquescence, 'un fleuve de chair' (i. 11 n.); Bacon's recourse to gymnastic posture and imagery; Bacon's use of washbasins, umbrellas, and mirrors as analogues of the circles and ovals which engulf and finally drain away the liquefying bodies of his subjects; Bacon's relation to Van Gogh and Cézanne; and a quite brilliant section on hysteria relating Bacon to Artaud and the *corps morcelé* where the body is reduced to zones and levels of pure sensation, bereft of limbs and traversed by violent forces. Deleuze also manages to complement existing criticism on Bacon (who is a painter who seems to attract a high level of critical writing) with original insights on established territory. Much, for example, has been written about Bacon's obsession with raw meat. The shock of early Bacon pictures in which butcher's meat is juxtaposed with, and then actually fused into, the body of the sitter, is still profoundly unnerving. *Painting, 1946* (ii, pl. 30; Museum of Modern Art, New York) has a black-suited figure with yellow buttonhole and head half-obscured by black umbrella, surrounded by bloody and glistening joints of meat, offal, and cleaved carcasses crucified at his back. In the legendary interviews with David Sylvester Bacon remarked:

Well of course, we are meat, we are potential carcasses. If I go into a butcher's shop I always think it's surprising that I wasn't there instead of the animal. But using the meat in that particular way is possibly like the way one might use the spine, because we are constantly seeing images of the human body through X-ray photographs and that obviously does alter the ways by which one can use the body.[1]

Deleuze begins by exploring this obsession in terms of Bacon's manifold attacks upon the symbolic and physical integrity of the human body. An ancient form of grotesque hybrid is the mutant combination of animal and human, and Deleuze begins from that traditional category: 'In place of formal correspondences, Bacon's paintings constitute a zone of perplexing obscurity (*indiscernabilité*) of indecidability, between human and animal . . . this objective zone of indecidability is already the whole body, but the body present as flesh or meat' (i. 19–20).

But Deleuze goes on to examine the dissociation of bone from flesh which is so marked in his figures and thereby pushes the discussion beyond the conventional categories of the grotesque. Bacon 'bones' his sitters before your eyes. Their bodies appear as flayed viscera, pulpy and twisted sacks of muscle and cartilage devoid of skeletal support. They are often tense, only held in place by some sudden spasm. Bones do appear, as in *Triptych, two figures lying on a bed with attendants, 1968* (ii, pl. 53; Museum of Modern Art, Tehran) and the exposed vertebrae in *Three figures and portrait, 1975* (ii, pl. 40; Tate Gallery, London), but *outside* the body so that they are transformed into a prosthetic exoskeleton, totally separate from the figures. For Deleuze this separation of bone from flesh is a major part of a strenuously demanding effort by Bacon to paint the pure sensation of hysteria, to 'directly touch the nervous system itself' as Bacon put it. His art is a presentation as much as a representation. Moving via Rilke and Artaud (and we might add Kafka in *Metamorphosis*, where exoskeletal form seems to

[1] David Sylvester, *The Brutality of Fact: Interviews with Francis Bacon*, 3rd enlarged edn. (London, 1987), 46.

have a related function in representing phobic loss of identity in animal/human mutation), Deleuze ascribes their dissociation to the corporeal registration of the hysterical moment in Bacon. In hysteria the body escapes itself, it nearly 'jumps out of its skin', voiding itself 'via the open mouth, the stomach, the anus, the throat' (i. 36). Unlike Salvador Dali, who also eviscerates the body of his subjects, reducing them to a melting and malleable viscosity propped up by a variety of contrived prosthetic devices, Bacon reinfuses his subjects with a hysterical, muscular intensity. They often have a gymnastic posture as though in torsion, wrenched into impossible positions. Prone, the curved figures are made to look as though they had been both discarded and carefully displayed at the same time, like victims of some appalling torture.

Deleuze is particularly fine in his formal analyses of these separate hysterical elements in Bacon's work, the rendering visible of those hidden, convulsive forces which seize the body in its flight from panic. 'The hysteric' wrote Freud, 'simply represses.' It falls to the body to expel those phobic monstrosities which the mind simply cannot acknowledge: they are voided, vomited, denied. In a sensationalist culture which perpetually inflates the value of shock (as Walter Benjamin clearly saw) Bacon is one of the very few artists to have ensnared the true visceral impression of the body's suction at the instant of *sursaut*, of its *mise en abîme*. In picture after picture, as the flesh metamorphoses into pigment and figures melt first into *figuration* and then swirl into pools of thickly coloured discharge, the space of abjection arcs out before us. Yet none of this tries to impress. Indeed sometimes, as in his portrait of George Dyer and Lucien Freud in 1967 (ii. 63; destroyed), Bacon even seems protective towards his sitters, infusing their tense bodies with a certain camp humour. Such instances are rare: for the most part Bacon bears witness to an 'excruciating carnality', to use Susan Sontag's term, which we thrust aside in order to live. Bacon paints extreme sensation but avoids the purely sensational into which commercial culture has all but dissolved that category. Deleuze rightly celebrates the particular intransigence of a painter whom he considers to have, miraculously, painted trauma without ever descending to the merely traumatic or to an exploited rhetoric of horror.

However, I emerged from Deleuze's book dazzled by fine analyses of specific paintings but finally disappointed by its overall judgement of the work. Surprisingly, given the breadth of his previous studies, Deleuze never satisfactorily connects Bacon's presentation of hysteria to cultural history. Disappointment grew as Deleuze seemed to find it more and more difficult to show the social significance of the formal analyses he produced. He writes with extraordinary insight about the interrelations of perception, form, and hysteria, but then lapses into either a vague and unconvincing humanism, a bland approbation of stoicism in the face of suffering, or into a diagnosis of Bacon's own pathological condition. Neither of these seems at all adequate to the depth of analysis offered of the *compositional* structure of the paintings. Deleuze never satisfactorily convinces us that the graphic portrayal of the hysterical moment is of general significance. This seems to be more than a mere imbalance in his study between analysis and judgement. It means that we are left with the uneasy sense that Deleuze is unable to find the categories in which he can think the intimate complicity between individual pathology, artistic form, and cultural meaning: from the author of *Anti-Oedipus* we surely expect precisely this as the informing strength of his project.

There is no such strength in *Logique de la sensation*. Indeed at pivotal moments Deleuze not only fails to connect, he offers a bland substitute of tragic existentialism as an ultimate reading of the paintings. Reverting to the worn clichés of Beckett and Kafka criticism, he falls into a rhetoric of existential humanism which is at odds with everything of verve and importance he has written in the past: 'We must pay to Bacon just as much as to Beckett or Kafka, this homage: they have created indomitable figures, intransigent in their resistance, their presence at the very moment when they were "representing" horror, mutilation, prosthesis, collapse or failure' (i. 42).[2]

With its stirring commonplaces, this passage does not even seem to me to be true. Most of Bacon's sitters, from the screaming Pope to the voiding, naked bodies of *Triptych* (1973, ii, pl. 29; collection Saul Sternberg, New York), exude sheer terror without a hint of compensatory stoicism to cheer the appalled viewer. The significance of Bacon's *œuvre* will not be found in Deleuze's book. We must look elsewhere.

Julia Kristeva in her recent book *Powers of Horror* provides a better guide to the overall cultural position of Bacon's work. Though she is primarily interested in Céline and does not write about Bacon, she provides a set of categories which have immediate power and resonance with respect to the hysterical basis of Bacon's paintings. Kristeva focuses upon 'abjection', a state of giddying instability and fear which is precipitated when the symbolic order regulating our identity unexpectedly collapses. Abjection denotes acute fear and disgust of a pathological kind, obsessive and recurrent in our lives, triggered by the 'abominable and filthy' with which we are unable to cope. Clearly linked to hysteria, abjection describes the panicky, twisting aside and away from those 'things' which burn and mutilate our self-possession. It is not so much repression in a classical sense as *rejection*, something more violent, jolting, and immediate in its carnivorous attack upon the body. It is an interior cataclysm which we repulse because it is in its turn 'repulsive'. Reactive, almost reflexive on account of uncontrollable nervous discharge, the abject feels split between a self and internalized otherness which s/he attempts to expel. This split or *Ich-spaltung* (Freud) destroys the fundamental subject–object boundary which both preserves subjective identity as such and keeps the world at bay. The abject is split between subject and object, neither fully an independent self nor com-

---

[2] 'On doit rendre à Bacon autant qu'à Beckett ou à Kafka l'hommage suivant: ils ont dressé des Figures indomptables, intransigeant par leur insistance, par leur présence, au moment même où ils "représentaient" l'horrible, la mutilation, la prothèse, la chute ou le raté.'

pletely determined by the objective realm, falling uncontrollably between both.

So much of what we do and say is silently governed in this respect by what we turn away from. The hysterical governance of waking life is vigilant and absolute. It is also intimate, enfolded in domestic commonplace, a flickering or a suction or a vertiginous arcing out amongst the ordinary rhythms of the day. Moments of falling; moments of loss; instants when time bloats and space distresses. All these things Bacon recalls and transfixes: the visceral core of abjection. In *Powers of Horror* Kristeva writes: 'It is thus not lack of cleanliness or health that causes abjection but what disturbs identity, system, order. What does not respect borders, positions, rules. The in-between, the ambiguous, the composite.'[3]

Abjection, like repression, is a function of social symbolic order and never merely a subjective matter. The grid of cultural definition is neither uniform nor seamless. In that vast, reticulated structure of signs which maps out our social world there are warps and vortices where subjectivity can be pitched unexpectedly into panic. Such *mises en abîme* are simultaneously historical and psychological. Never merely individual, they nevertheless convulse the individual, slewing the body as it drops between the hard edges of social order. Bodily discharge, raw meat, prosthetic devices, crawling insects, forms of the *grotesque*, these perilous sumps of ambiguity have a certain regularity in every culture. We discover them wherever an object, practice, or symbol destabilizes the primary binary pairings of a group or society. The more we uncover about the binary structures of culture the more evident it becomes that any chronic disruption of these dyads can become *traumatic*, in a strict sense, for a subject. Though Freud theorized the traumatic disruption of the maternal/paternal and male/female dyads and endowed them with privileged status, there is good reason to suppose that the failed mediation of other fundamental binary oppositions in a culture may be of considerable, perhaps even equal,

---

[3] Julia Kristeva, *Powers of Horror: An Essay on Abjection*, trans. Leon S. Roudiez (New York, 1982), 4.

consequence. Wherever we find abjection we will discover a failed mediation of traumatic proportions in the signifying system. We will also discover the provision of various procedures for coping with this failure—modes of taboo, displacement, reification, and repression. When *these* fail we are left with unmediated abjection, an intensity of terror almost without limit.

The Sartrean 'viscous', so apt for Bacon's figures, can now be understood and placed within a more comprehensive perspective, and one that is of considerable explanatory power in the aesthetic field. Viscosity designates the unstable mediation of solid and liquid, related both to bodily function and to ontological category. Like the skin on boiled milk, a primary opposition between solid and liquid (flesh ('skin') and milk) melts into a repulsive, coagulated substance allied to, yet alien from, both. (If the infant emerges from weaning having failed to securely mediate the flesh/milk opposition then the skin on milk is likely to be distressing even to the point of vomiting. Melanie Klein's work would undoubtedly offer insights into the aetiology of this common domestic abjection.) In order to cope with this substance we have to repress one pole of the binary opposition: there are those who discard the skin as 'not milk'; there are those who drink it down as part of the liquid. Those who can do neither fail to mediate the opposition and are overwhelmed by the presence of what they see as a disgusting, indeterminate slime. It is not too difficult, once the condition of failed mediation is understood, to map out the perilous sites of potential abjection within a culture.

Viscosity is of immense importance in Bacon's painting and indeed in modern art as a whole. Our culture seems to be particularly sensitive to the opposition between hard and soft and evokes this opposition to control areas of potential difficulty and threat: along its borders with transgressive sexuality it invokes a hard-core/soft-core distinction and along its borders with intimidating new technology it does the same, invoking a hardware/software distinction. Such patterns are not accidental. Much modern art appears to fetishize viscosity as a grotesque indeterminacy between 'hard' forms and liquid substance. Deleuze's analysis of Bacon's obsessive separation of flesh from bone can be seen in a wider perspective of cultural abjection in which both hard/soft and raw/cooked dyads are displayed and disrupted. Indeed the 'hysteria' of Bacon's art is a compound abjection, an extension of the traditional artistic grotesque into new areas of subverted mediation. Bacon carnivalizes the deep polarities which order cultural identity. Whereas traditional carnival turned the world upside-down in a comic and communal inversion of the binary oppositions regulating society, Bacon and modernism turn the world inside out rather than upside-down. Like the Beauborg Centre in Paris, Bacon's subjects are eviscerated and disembowelled, displaying on the outside what is normally hidden within. Bone and flesh confront each other or remain distressingly and inertly juxtaposed. Mushy, coagulated forms tumesce and slump; bodies churn and spew. It is impossible to decide whether the pale flesh of his subjects is membrane, shroud, or carcass. The inside is evacuated to the outside.

Lévi-Strauss explored the categorical unease about uncooked flesh expressed by South American tribes in their myths. *The Raw and the Cooked* reveals raw meat as an oddly disconcerting substance, enough by itself to make some of us nauseous. Whilst it remains uncooked it occupies a treacherously ambiguous position as 'flesh', too close to 'that which eats' and too far from 'that which is eaten'. It threatens far too many primary dyadic oppositions—dead/alive, eater/eaten, inside/outside, body/food, animal/human. Amusing no doubt, almost touching, that a painter named Bacon should be obsessed with depicting dead meat. The cooked and the raw. If ever there were scope for a deconstruction of 'the proper name' it is *that* name: Francis Bacon. It could never mark anything other than a lack of identity, a dispersal of nomination rather than a fixing and in-gathering. Doubly compromised—firstly by the fame of his illustrious relative, which dubbed him ineluctably as a latecomer, and secondly compromised by a stupid pun, 'Francis Bacon' could never designate a stable identity. If our own proper name remains, for most of us, a fragile self-containment, for the painter it was already, at the outset, another's name and a kind of pig meat. If raw flesh designates an ancient site of abjection, an instability of substance threatening the symbolic order and hence identity as such, it is reasonable and fitting that Bacon should project his own loss of identity in the same symbolic terms.

Meat, especially pig meat, was of course the symbolic centre of carnival (*carne-levare* probably derives from the 'taking up of meat' as both food and sex). The fact that Bacon gives it such prominence in his painting flavours the notion (adopted by Kristeva from Bakhtin) that modern art is often 'carnivalesque'. That's to say it destabilizes and subverts the governing forms of order in society through a violent celebration of the body, dirt, eating, drinking, and sexuality. 'Low' things are made 'high', normally repressed categories of behaviour are afforded powerful release. We can express this more accurately by saying that, traditionally, carnival is a ritual period in which repressed terms of the primary dyadic structures in society are foregrounded, celebrated, and allowed to destabilize the symbolic order in a festive riot of ambivalence. Men dress as women, women as men; people dress as animals and also devour them; filth replaces incense, the holy places become scenes of sexual play. Inside and outside, high and low, open and closed, finished and unfinished—a number of basic binary oppositions coding the organizational structure of society are deliberately distressed. Normal mediations are suspended or convulsed. Opposites become mixed and confused in the universal adoption of the grotesque. Orifices, particularly the gaping mouth, emphasize the open, unfinished, receptive nature of the body at carnival, its daily proximity to flesh and to dung.

Bacon's paintings represent all these things and indeed can be seen to be structured precisely on the grotesque tradition which developed in close relation to carnival. But Bacon offers a morbid carnival of distress and defilement which, lacking the ambivalent laughter, hierarchical inversion, and communal celebration of traditional carnival, emerges as diagnostic rather than cathartic. As such it is all the more likely to be read off—as indeed Deleuze does—as an index of the existential misery of the isolated bourgeois soul. It is an example of what Bakhtin called 'carnival of the night', in which the utopian and the politically subversive aspects of folk culture are eroded so that the carnivalesque becomes interiorized and individualized, related to private terror, isolation, and insanity rather than to robust, communal celebration. It becomes related then, to *abjection*, and Bacon's paintings reveal more clearly than any other modern example the intimate connection between carnivalized structure and hysterical abjection in the modern period.

The core of Bacon's work is in the grotesque tradition which Thomas Mann called 'the most striking feature and most genuine style of modern art'. Within the grotesque (which always emerges from a hybridization of binary opposites) Bacon's work develops a particular modality of what might be called 'the prosthetic grotesque'.

Perhaps it was Breugel who first captured the terror of prosthesis—the surgical substitution of a mechanical adjunct to replace a part of the human body destroyed or diseased. The taboos of our culture have ensured that the 'prosthetic grotesque' has hitherto been more or less invisible as a cultural category. Repression has both reified and fragmented its underlying process as one of the major modalities of the grotesque tradition in Western art. Yet as the prosthetic gradually cedes to the bionic, a retrospective sense of the historical importance of the mechanical/human dyad is made visible in that *après coup* which seems to dictate that we truly see cultural forms only as they begin to fade. Conventional histories of the grotesque have familiarized the human/plant and human/animal mutations which have been the traditional stuff of grotesque art. Yet the human/mechanical is a third kind of perverse inmixing with its own discrete but related history at least as significant as the other two.

To enter this zone where nature is travestied by mechanical contraption is to encounter a specific kind of terror, a terror which resides entirely in what Kristeva calls abjection. The terror is moreover exorbitant when measured against the original loss or debility. That's to say, prosthetic objects— crutches, wigs, false teeth, spectacles, callipers, wheelchairs, artificial limbs—create a phobic aura quite other than that of the accident or illness which necessitated their use, such that, strangely, the horror of prosthesis has only a minimal relation to the fear of ill health. It is an irrational, hysterical fear different in depth and kind from the fear of sickness.

Phenomenologically, protheses exude a stubborn individualism (this is one reason why there is a formidable resistance on the part of culture to see or perceive these assorted objects as a set). Each is marked by a uniqueness, a 'thingyness' which makes each *more than object*, unassimilable either to other objects or to the body itself. Neither fully 'out there' nor fully 'in here', every prosthesis is a bit of a character, defined by its parodic duplication of the limb or organ it replaces. It is defined not only by an absence, which it announces by its difference, but also by a deficiency, which it ostensibly makes up. But of course it never does fully make up. It tends rather to agonize the recall, distort the echo, and thereby emphasize the aesthetic loss by the banality of its pragmatism, by its naked endurance as pure *use-value*.

Although we may trace the prosthetic grotesque through Van Gogh, Goya, Callot, Breugel, and Bosch, the particular conjunction of medical and mechanical knowledges in the nineteenth and early twentieth centuries determine that period as overwhelmingly more significant than any other. Not only the art of Bacon, but that of Ensor, de Chirico, Tanguy, Dali, Picasso, Ernst, Klee, and Weber would be unrecognizable without it. For self-evident reasons the aftermath of the First World War saw the most intensive and widespread application of the prosthetic grotesque. Not only in the literal depiction of the crippled and permanently damaged soldiers who filled the streets of Europe from 1915 onwards and who fill the embittered canvases of Otto Dix, George Grosz, and other *Neue Sachlichkeit* painters, but also in emergent forms of abstraction less nearly associated with the literal horrors of war; cubism, expressionism, vorticism, futurism. It was Bacon who exploited the power of the prosthetic grotesque most relentlessly. His canvases not only frequently depict prosthetic objects, these objects become content-correlatives of abjection as it destroys the subject–object separation necessary for normal psychological functions. Prosthesis becomes a mode of spatial and symbolic reification. I have written above of prosthetic *objects*, but in truth prostheses are not objects as other objects are. They occupy and occlude a disturbing middle ground, disrupting the clear mediation of subject and object. Ontologically unstable, they can be definitively claimed neither by the body nor by the world and they thereby violate the coherence and integrity of the body-image. They are the very stuff of abjection.

In Bacon's work the prosthetic grotesque cuts across the separate realms of cultural history and individual psychology to reveal the hystericalized body as its *social instance*. It is the prosthetic grotesque which reveals the limits of otherness and of identity in machine culture—it is striking how, in the first machine age, there was a massive transformation in the binaryisms of the grotesque, from plant/human and animal/human pairings to human/machine dyads. Curiously, this grotesque form was rarely situated or imaged in a factory. There the relation of man (but not woman) to machine was sufficiently clearly mediated by masculinity—the muscularity of the male worker and the army of labour—within a patriarchal symbolic order. It was rather in those discourses where the mechanical threat to the integrity of body-image was both more privatized and deeply unsettling that the grotesque found its place, utilizing medicine, surgery, dentistry, optics, and photography, discourses where the intimacy of reification was most intense.

Bacon's fascination for these discourses is well documented. His fond recollections about books on X-ray technique, diseases of the mouth, Muyerbridge's photographic record of motion, and certain kinds of apparatus are recorded in the interviews with David Sylvester. Modern art reveals a morbid fascination for that surface zone, close to, or in contact with the body, where mechanical or technical intrusion is most disturbing, where flesh, membrane, and metal coalesce or repel each other. Bacon's spectacles, umbrellas, and false teeth have this in common with Magritte and Dali, though Bacon's work is entirely devoid of the dandy showmanship of the latter.

Bacon nearly always surrounds his portrayed sitters with claustrophobic scaffolding, handrails, mirrors, blindcords, dangling lightbulbs, apparatus, contraptions which simultaneously confine and support them. These are a generalized extension of the prosthetic framing in which he employs spectacles (he is obsessed with the famous still from Eisenstein's *Potemkin* in which the nurse is shown in close-up on the Odessa steps, her spectacles splintered into one eye and her mouth agape), false teeth, crutches, splints, and hospital beds as instruments of abjection. These 'hard' forms jut out against the soft plasticity of the human body to produce an effect analogous to the 'boning' of his sitters, the separation of bone from flesh noted by Deleuze. A curious feature of composition in Bacon which I feel is part of the same prosthetic configuration is the use of small, hard arrows imposed upon the painting—what Bacon tellingly refers to as 'rivets'. These 'rivets', pointing a direction of force in a diagrammatic, technical way as if taken from a plan or drawing, have the precise effect of symbolic prosthesis in which *technē* coerces and guides the disordered body. These little arrows of instruction, these rivets, both attack and give direction, suggesting an implicit inadequacy or helplessness in the sitter.

The prosthetic grotesque assumes an alienation of structure from substance. It juxtaposes hard against soft, geometry and linearity against flesh. The tendency within modernism has been to segregate those elements severely, to set abstract expression over against action painting. Within the modern tradition the development of abstract art has pursued a kind of purist rigour in conscious opposition not only to representational art, but to substance, matter, and the process of painting as such. Deleuze wishes to celebrate what he takes to be Bacon's superiority to the (then current) options of abstract expressionism on the one hand and action painting on the other. In agreeing with Deleuze that this is one of the positive achievements of Bacon, I would also want to point out that it is a natural correlative of the prosthetic grotesque. Bacon's paintings are figurative and representational, yet *what* they figure is a process, an act of graphic expulsions. We witness body becoming paint (*Triptych*, August 1972, ii, pl. 70; Tate Gallery, London), a dissolution of representation into the substance of paint itself, with its blotches, smears, and scrapings. This liquefaction not only utilizes all the tactile resources of action painting, its exhilaration, energy, and transgressive indulgence in the fecal smear; it also goes beyond it by *representation*, by painting figures dissolving into paint which become, in turn, new figures. Unlike Pollock, Bacon always has the possibility of representation not only *of* the paint, but *through* the paint, of its corporeal, purgative joy—its coils, heaps, and bunches, its splats and explosions (see *Triptych, Studies of the human body*, 1970, ii, pl. 22; Marlborough International Fine Art).

Though it would be hard to deny the excremental mischief in Bacon which enables him to display the 'soft' spectrum of modernism in action, his greater achievement is to have set the soft against the hard—to have brought action painting into a dialogue with abstraction on the site of grotesque realism. Thus the *composition* of Bacon's paintings, particularly the interior spaces and the prosthetic apparatus, reveal his full and self-conscious adaptation of abstract, geometric blocks of colour, shape, and line. Large flat circles and squares resolved in two dimensions mock the eye in its effort to place the sitters in rooms with conventional perspective. The empty cubes and trapezia, the abstract curves, linearities, and constructivist fragments of furniture are demystified in Bacon—denied their transcendental aspiration towards pure form.

Too often abstract modernism takes refuge in its purism and its rationalism. It is safe art. In Bacon the formalism and aesthetic purity of his contemporaries are estranged, recontextualized as props to the convulsed bodies of his sitters. Within the powerful emotional field of the canvas these abstract forms become citations. They often appear embarrassed by their beauty, external to the dramatic focus of the pictures (*Tryptych*, 1976, ii, pl. 27; private collection, France). Suspended within the composition as quoted objects these abstract forms are shown up as aestheticizing strategies. Bacon dialogizes abstract expressionism, subverting its precious order and sanitized form by placing it beside flesh, raw meat, and the human body under extreme duress.

In *Triptych* (1970; National Gallery of Australia, Canberra), the sitter in the left- and right-hand panels, fully clothed in one and naked in the other, is perched on a gymnastic trapeze which playfully echoes the work of the constructivists: bold blocks of black and brown, flat discs, and saucers of sombre colour are suspended on a few straight filaments. In the middle panel two lovers curled up together are held aloft on a large blue-mauve oval which cannot be resolved by the eye into a vertical or horizontal plane. It is as if Bacon had set out to master and then interanimate the major currents of modernism—figural representation, action painting, and abstract expressionism—so as to produce a triangulated tension from the essential strengths of all three. This aspect of Bacon, his aesthetic combat with his contemporaries, seems to me one of his real achievements. Not only has he captured and adapted the best of their techniques, he has overcome their sectarian purism to reinvest painting with a passion and tension often absent from each tendency on its own.

In the end, however, it is hysterical abjection which dominates the pictures. Bacon 'presents' through the prosthetic grotesque the long night's carnival of capitalism in the first machine age. In 1928 Breton and Aragon declared hysteria to be 'the greatest poetical discovery of the twentieth century', and indeed Freud's *Dora*, read against the grain, now seems to many of us to stand as a key text at the opening of our century. Yet the artistic discovery of hysteria offered revelation without cure. It provided a distressing, privileged glimpse of the phobic substratum of a social formation chronically unable to manage its communal symbolic life. Bacon's solitary abjects bear witness to a society bereft of the basic ritual forms necessary to mediate cultural production: hysteria became the most authentic bourgeois equivalent to the carnivalesque. This is the lasting social indictment at the heart of Bacon's wager: that the most fitting poetic image of his culture, the diagnostic ideal for his age, was his own hysteria.

Afterword

JACQUELINE ROSE

At the very end of Allon White's first book, *The Uses of Obscurity*, he comments on the recurrent phrase used, in Henry James's late novel *The Wings of the Dove*, to describe Milly Theale's acquiescence in death: 'She has turned her face to the wall.' In this phrase, he writes, 'death and the deepest processes of James's art are brought together in a delicate euphemism'. The image of the 'turned back', and the 'question that comes from behind', punctuate James's writing and Allon White's exegesis. Recurrent in both, they stand for a knowledge that can only be approached obliquely, a secret offered and withheld.

If death is the most appropriate—the final—image for this form of knowledge, writing is also what is being talked about. In this account, modernist fiction has produced a new writer with a private history—an interiority—which he himself is incapable of grasping completely, something which he will not, but also cannot, disclose. Neither 'contingent' nor 'intentional', the famous obscurities of modernism are rather 'moments when knowledge threatens to destroy something so fundamentally constitutive of the fiction-making that its clear and direct revelation would silence the discourse'. Novelists tend 'compulsively' to return to moments or episodes which 'haunt or hurt them'—it is this 'painfulness which coaxes forth their written elaborations or misremembrances': 'It is because certain things are opaque to the novelists themselves that the novels are written.' Paradoxically then, knowledge would be the death of fiction, but death is also the best image we have for that form of not-knowing which keeps the writing alive.

In his essay on Dickens's *Bleak House*, Allon White describes the moment when Esther sees Lady Dedlock's face: it was 'like a broken glass to me, in which I saw scraps of old remembrance'. In this instance, rediscovering a lost link is, he writes, 'like the recovery of some precious object lost under secrets or pressed back out of site'. Memory here is restorative, and the attempt to restore lines of communication and information is what drives the narrative on. As if the novel's life, like that of its characters, depended on opening up channels which are blocked throughout the story (stagnant river, bureaucratic petrification and disease). Those who obstruct the flow destroy others as well as themselves—Tulkinghorn, 'a hoarder diseased by a canker of rust', Lady Dedlock, frozen—deadlocked—into aristocratic stasis. In this case, not to uncover the past is what kills. Recovery is benign—it opens up human contact and lets the rivers flow.

The question of memory—whether it destroys or saves—is one strand that runs through Allon White's writing, linking the critical pieces to the autobiography. At its simplest, it is a recurrent theme in many of the texts. More important is the way this theme seems in itself to be part of a remarkable commentary on the relation between private and public discourse, between the most intimate language of the psyche and the most formal, theoretical, of academic speech. In that first book, the art of criticism is avowedly persecutory, a 'cat-and-mouse game' in which the critic carries out on his chosen writers the very form of reading which they have most carefully guarded against. Interpretation contains 'the possibility of harm against them', just as inside the novels—most obviously in Henry James—disclosure does not bring its own reward. 'The honest consciousness drifts into trouble'—by which he means the characters who reveal their secrets, but also the probing of the critic, hunting down his quarry in a siege whose relentless one-way scrutiny is the only way—it will become more and more explicit—the critic can conceal himself, the only way he can in turn survive. One of the most extraordinary things about reading these texts, then, is to watch this process turn around—as the critic gradually comes to direct that very same form of pained and painful attention on to his own obscurities, the episodes which 'haunt or hurt' him, the secrets of his own past and inner world. At this level, the message seems to be clear: the critic hunts the writer because he is fleeing—but finally will have to track down—himself.

In the previously unpublished piece 'Why Am I a Literary Critic?', written two years before he fell ill with leukaemia, Allon White writes about the terror of disclosure:

I am aware that this, for me, is dangerous. It is all a matter of distance. Always I am underdistanced, too close to memory, too close to my past. When I write therefore I write with the hand and the eye of my other to guide me and keep me safe . . . I am a critic because there in the writing out of the other the distance is perfect and I am safe.

That 'writing out of the other' is ambiguous: writing from the place—with the hand and eye, as he puts it—of the other; but also writing out, cancelling, ejecting, the other who—it is an inherent part of the mechanism—unfailingly returns: 'how *close* now, how perilous the thing must be, the stamping of the beast upon the shore'.

This beast is memory, the personal trauma of childhood he writes about so vividly in the autobiographical fragment 'Too Close to the Bone' (the image of the beast on the shore perfectly captures—as well as the threat—the dilemma, the enraged hesitation of memory, angry for entry and poised on a threshold it cannot cross). Yet it is hard not to read it too as his approaching illness: 'Yet, and yet. For some reason as I approach the age of three and thirty something is coming closer to me out of my own past and I know that I shall be a literary critic for very little longer.' Writing his autobiography, he retrieves the fragment of his early novel whose hero dies of malaria in Sardinia in the swamps he has gone to drain, together with the memory of his sister's death by drowning when she (and he) was a young child. Although his illness might be pure 'biological malignancy'; 'yet, the prescience of my fiction disturbs me. Malaria. Leukaemia.

Disease of the blood. A life which, at every crisis, turned broodingly to images of shady ponds and stagnant waters, death by drowning.'

This, then, is the scene which 'haunts' and 'hurts', coaxing forth in him, as in those early modern writers, 'misremembrances' now being—slowly and painfully—undone: 'I see water and the lilies and the reeds and the weeds and unless I can understand all that then I am as dead.' ('Why Am I a Literary Critic?') Revelation is the only salvation, the only chance of life. But then he adds: 'I have come too close. I have deadened myself with that last word. I killed my pain and my memory. I typed myself dead.' Memory is an equivocal blessing. In the process of retrieval, he kills the living nerve of his own recollection, and 'dies'. Like the critical activity which overlays and conceals it, memory can in itself be the great persecutor: the voices and faces he calls up from the past 'will execute me, of that I am certain. This will be, in some sense, a death.' In this sense, Allon White writes along the edge of what appears at moments as an insurmountable difficulty ('along the inner edge of hysteria *all the time* without, up to now ever knowing it')—how to negotiate the twin dangers of memory, the felt peril of memory whether evaded or confronted, pushed away or embraced?

It is, however, too easy to see this in exclusively personal, psychological terms, too easy to turn that extraordinary arc that stretches from the death of Milly Theale to the autobiography into a merely symptomatic text. When Allon White writes of the death of Lucas Arnow, 'It is really within himself that the poison develops', it seems as if this is pure diagnosis, death the consequence of the failure to confront the inner recesses of the mind: 'It is precisely the *absence* of magical vision and rage within him, or at least their deep and irrecoverable repression, which cankers his soul.' Yet between these two sentences lies this one: 'His entirely laudable . . . petit-bourgeois sense of purpose and identity are no match for the miasmic forces welling up inside him.' Arnow is a technician who comes to drain the marshes. The reference here is to a legacy of early bourgeois technology which is historical and precise. Among the notes for the novel is this passage: 'The dyke and calculation, drainage and mathematical precision were all part of the same bourgeois nexus. Holland, Dutch interiors, precise, clean, clear, representative, all impossible without the dykes. The dykes and the drains, the end of Feudalism, the coming of petit-bourgeois land geometry.' 'Are you', he asks at another point in his notes, 'writing a completely negative fiction of bourgeois technological failure?'

So does Lucas Arnow die of malaria, or of his petit-bourgeois purpose and identity, of a failing, inherent in bourgeois culture, to match the forces it confronts? More, is it the attempt of that culture to tidy the (Dutch) interiors, to clean up the swamps and the streets, that creates the problem by *making* these forces malign? Running clearly through Allon White's writing is another strand—as well known as his discussion of modernist writing—which parallels and interweaves with that encounter with memory and death. And that is the history of the suppression of carnival, of the grotesque body, of excrement, smell, and dirt—rituals and symbols of an earlier and more heterogeneous cultural moment, not so much lost as pushed underground. It is, he writes, in his essay on the painter Francis Bacon, 'the lasting social indictment at the heart of Bacon's wager: that the most fitting poetic image of his culture, the diagnostic ideal for his age, was his own hysteria'. ('OH! How I understand those awful paintings!'—'Why Am I a Literary Critic?') Only when the grotesque body became pure representation or spectacle did the cultural energies it once carried become unmanageable, returning as foreign body through the unconscious of the bourgeois subject, welling up inside his body and mind: 'the mundane only has to flicker a little and it arches out into hysterical instability' ('Pynchon'). And what leads to and underlies this form of representation (the grotesque as image or word) also, at one level, signals its collapse: 'The interior terror and subliminal anxiety which turn our bodies into the battleground of our fears also make the effort of controlled representation almost impossible'

('Bacon'). In this context, the founding achievement of modern civilized existence—the draining of the marshes—is what sows the seed of that same civilization's malaise. If memory is dangerous, then, it is because bourgeois culture has made the body abject, turned smell—marsh, swamp, sewer—into a foe.

In *The Politics and Poetics of Transgression*, Allon White's second book, written with Peter Stallybrass, it is central to the argument that this history, no less than the world of personal memory and trauma from which it is inseparable, carries with it its own fantasy of disclosure, its own fascination–repulsion for something which also belongs to an order of truth. So, when Mayhew writes in the 1960s about cleansing the city, uncovering its sins and its dirt, and focuses on the streets and roads on the surface and the hidden sewers and drains underneath, 'he repeats one of the dominant tropes of Western metaphysics: truth lies hidden behind a veil. But "truth" is now conceived materially as excrement.' In Conrad's short story 'The Return'—in a passage cited in *The Uses of Obscurity*—the crowd of a West End theatre scatters 'with the hurried air of men fleeing . . . from something suspected and concealed—like truth or pestilence'. More than metaphorical, that link between truth and pestilence operates in these texts as a fully social indictment. Thus Allon White's writing diagnoses the ills of petit-bourgeois purpose and perhaps also his own illness—culture, and body *in extremis*, we might say.

It is, then, one of the achievements of this set of writings to show in its fabric (as well as to take as its explicit theoretical argument) how tightly the personal is bound to the cultural, the way an individual subjectivity inherits, and is made by, a history beyond all conscious imagining and control. When Allon White remembers his 'father's dirty, oily hands . . . rough and smelly when they touch me' and determines never to have such hands, when he leaves a world which he recalls first through its *smells* (sulphur, cod-liver oil, and stagnant pools), he is starting out on a journey—from the garage to the academy, from dirt to refinement, from the 'fuckpissshit' of the favourite garage-hand of his childhood to the 'dismal sacred word' of high culture—which enacts in miniature the cultural and literary history he then writes. Except that in his writing he makes the journey in reverse—from the 'infinite repertoire of civilization' and its 'will to refinement' (*The Uses of Obscurity*) to the grotesque (*The Politics and Poetics of Transgression*), from academy to memory, from distance to proximity, from outside the body to its most intimate dissolution (the 'boning' of Francis Bacon's painted subjects and 'Too Close to the Bone').

One way of reading this trajectory, therefore, might be to see it as an almost historic destiny—it is at least one way that he seems to write it—as he takes up into his body, succumbs to and falls ill with, the malignancy of a culture he himself diagnosed and whose most refined laurels he coveted and won. The stream of a partially forgotten history erupting into the blood. It would be wrong, however, to judge from this—to read him as judging—that the critical activity is only false, since this activity, certainly in the theories on which he most consistently draws (Julia Kristeva, Mikhail Bakhtin), is the way back to that history, one central means through which it can be retrieved and retold. It is an intrinsic part of the critical, as much as the personal, project to lay bare the premises of high critical language, to write the history of its dismal pretension, and turn it back on itself. Theory, as these writings demonstrate so brilliantly, can also go underground.

In a central chapter of *The Politics and Poetics of Transgression*, he describes the emergence of the bourgeois writer, who elevates himself above the crowd, observing from a place of untouchable superiority the spectacle, grime, and debris of the city streets. According to an almost formal logic, the paradigm for this new writer seems to split along an axis: 'I write/You stink' (writing as 'an idealized space of consciousness being systematically scoured')—the opposition between the 'I' and the 'You', the knowing, transcendent discrimination of the first, is as crucial as the more obvious binary of the literary/plebeian worlds which it supports. That this 'I' is a subterfuge has been one of the most persistent themes of the theoretical tradition on which Allon White draws. This 'I' is vulnerable in direct proportion to its effort to get on top of the world. Hence the epigraph from D. H. Lawrence to the article on Julia Kristeva: 'How could he say "I" when he was something new and unknown, not himself at all? This I, this old formula of the age, was a dead letter'; and this quotation from the notes to the novel: 'My "I" is the force which draws circle upon circle on the water when the stone has long lain slumbering on the bottom of the lake.' Once more, the point about cultural and linguistic form carries, barely concealed, the history of a more acutely felt trauma—dead letter, water, depths.

Over and again, it is these almost uncanny moments of parallelism which are so striking. Writing on Wordsworth as he surveys, from 'his perspective of visionary aloofness', the city dwellers at the fair, 'slaves . . . of low pursuits', Allon White quotes these lines from *The Prelude*:

> Living among the same perpetual flow
> Of trivial objects, melted and reduced
> To one identity, by differences
> That have no law, no meaning and no end.

What threatens, alongside but finally far more than the social abjection, is boundaries melting, objects merging, discrimination (taste, differences) dissolved into 'perpetual flow'. Compare this language with the way he describes the place deep inside him where he lodged the 'hysterical body' of his identification with the sister who drowned: 'Nothing can be held steady enough for language in this place; things flicker and slide, shapes loom and melt away.'

Identity and language fall apart, our finest discriminations are a ruse, the politeness of culture a ploy. How much—the question seems to be—can the 'I' afford, physically, psychically, historically, to remember? What are the forms of duping, of participant ignorance, in which we all share? Among the notes for the novel is this comment: 'Cultural and fictional forms motivate us to the degree that their function to motivate remains completely concealed. *The authority of culture and fiction is a function of participant ignorance.*' At these points in his writing, Allon White seems again to touch the limits of disclosure, issuing his own note of caution to the challenges to propriety constantly issued throughout these texts. What would it mean to 'unveil' completely these devious modes of self-fashioning, these collectively and personally sustained forms of ignorance, if what we discover on the other side is total breakdown, the loss of the very forms through which they can be, at least partially, known?

Is it possible to write one's own death? It was hard to avoid some such impression, or at least a sense of anticipatory mourning, as I read through Allon White's work, published and unpublished, the notes for his novel, his collection of quotations inscribed on to cards:

And, after all, is it not *always* apparent that only those who are alive can really die.

> My end draws nigh; 'tis time that I were gone.
> Make broad thy shoulders to receive my weight,
> And bear me to the margin; yet I fear
> My wound hath taken cold, and I shall die.
>
> (Tennyson)

But if he was doing so, it seems to me that he made that death 'monumental' (his last research during his illness was on memorials and tombstones)—inscribed it into the cycle of history which produced him, but without ever losing, and more and more rejoining, the uniquely personal myth of an individual destiny. If nothing else, and they are a lot more besides, these texts provide a unique testimony of how a critical project draws its energy from what comes before and behind, history and psyche furiously working themselves out together on the page.

Bibliography

1977   'L'Éclatement du sujet: The Work of Julia Kristeva', in 'Exposition and Critique of Julia Kristeva', stencilled occasional paper (General Series: SP No. 49), Centre for Contemporary Cultural Studies, University of Birmingham.

1978   'Language and Location in *Bleak House*', *Critical Quarterly*, 20.

1981   *The Uses of Obscurity: The Fiction of Early Modernism* (London).

1983   '"The Dismal Sacred Word": Academic Language and the Social Reproduction of Seriousness', *LTP: Journal of Literature Teaching Politics*, 2.

1984   'Bakhtin, Sociolinguistics, and Deconstruction', in *The Theory of Reading*, ed. Frank Gloversmith (Brighton).

1985   'Hysteria and the End of Carnival: Festivity and Bourgeois Neurosis', *Semiotica*, 54/1–2.

1986   With Peter Stallybrass:
        The Politics and Poetics of Transgression (London).

1987–8 'The Struggle over Bakhtin: Fraternal Reply to Robert Young', *Cultural Critique*, 8 (Winter 1987–8).

1989   *Too Close to the Bone: Fragments of an Autobiography*, first published in *London Review of Books*, 4 May 1989, and *Raritan Review*, 8 (Spring 1989); reprinted in book form by the *London Review of Books* (1991).

1993   'Why Am I a Literary Critic?', written *c*.1984, first published in this volume.

1993   'Prosthetic Gods in Atrocious Places: Gilles Deleuze/Francis Bacon', written 1983, first published in this volume.

Index

Note: Allon White is abbreviated to AW